The Falling Sickness

for Frances

Russell Edson

Russell Edson

The Falling Sickness

A Book of Plays

A New Directions Book

ACKNOWLEDGMENTS

The plays collected here, although having been published separately before, have, the author hopes, been brought closer to his best effort by extensive revisions; this, with the other tasks attached to preparing a book for the finality of print, represents one of the completed projects undertaken during the period of Fellowship granted him by the John Simon Guggenheim Memorial Foundation, here acknowledged with grateful thanks.

Some of the material in this volume first appeared in *Theatre Experiment*, edited by Michael Benedikt (New York, Doubleday, 1967), *New Directions in Prose and Poetry* (Nos. 23 and 26), and *Tri-Quarterly*.

Manufactured in the United States of America
First published clothbound and as New Directions Paperbook 389 in 1975
Published simultaneously in Canada by McClelland & Stewart, Ltd.

Library of Congress Cataloging in Publication Data

Edson, Russell.
  The falling sickness.

  (A New Directions Book)
  CONTENTS: The falling sickness.—The crawlers.—The children.—Ketchup.
  I. Title.
PS3509.D583F3   1975   812'.5'2   74–23986
ISBN 0–8112–0561–4
ISBN 0–8112–0562–2 pbk.

New Directions Books are published for James Laughlin by New Directions Publishing Corporation, 333 Sixth Avenue, New York 10014

Contents

The Falling Sickness

The Falling Sickness

This is a seven-part entertainment concerning a father and mother, both middle-aged, and their thirty- or forty-year-old son and his twin sister, who is played by the same actor who plays the son.

The action takes place in a shabby kitchen, where the misunderstood past is ritualized and repeated as kitchen vaudeville.

The protagonist is the collective past of this family, which each member attempts to "act out" and free.

Any resemblance to persons living or dead may not be purely coincidental, therefore these characters are presented in their universal pronouns.

PART ONE

[*The son walks out and falls; gets up and walks a few steps and falls again; gets up and goes to a window and screams; falls, gets up and walks staggeringly to the front of the stage, and looks longingly into the audience as though expecting someone. He stands there for a moment, then screams, falls, and is still.*]

FATHER [*offstage*]: Should we dance?

MOTHER [*offstage*]: No, no, just walk on!

[*They enter the stage.*]

FATHER [*with a vague gesture*]: Should we curtsy?

MOTHER [*wearing a large white apron, scrutinizing the audience*]: We don't have to be afraid to walk into our own kitchen, even if one of the walls seems to be full of people.

FATHER: People?!—People in our walls?! I suppose they think I'll dance for them. [*He sticks his tongue out at the audience, and then turns to his wife.*] When did we first come here? Or were we always here? . . . I can't remember ever remembering anything. Did I ever remember anything? . . . Or, did we arrive here like epileptics, traveling through the midnight of some unconscious joy? Yes, yes, I remember! I said, look, look, out of everything in the universe, a kitchen! We've awakened in a kitchen!

MOTHER: You did not! You thought you were in a bathroom. You looked at the stove and said, "Ah, a toilet with fire!" I said, stop it or I'll kill you! And you, avoiding the subject because you always hated to think about dying, said, "Ooo, what a lovely white toilet full of ice!" I said, please! please! PLEASE! . . . Oh, how I hate you!

FATHER: Did you say *love?* Isn't that one of those dirty jokes? [*False laughter*] Ho ho, ha ha, he he, what a dirty rotten filthy joke. No, no, I'm much too serious for such unfixed, unconcentrated, wandering, desultory, trifling, frivolous, flippant, blah, blah, blah, blah, blah, blah!

MOTHER: Our son . . .

FATHER: Our son NOT! Shall we dance?!

MOTHER: *Shall we dance?* . . . Didn't I take my clothes off in front of you once?

FATHER: But, your head, you didn't undress your head.

MOTHER: My head? My head is where I make up things to do.

FATHER: Please do not make up anything to do against me.

MOTHER [*shrilly*]: Our son!

FATHER: Something else.

MOTHER: Thirty or forty years . . . Exhibit A.

FATHER: A criminal assault upon my eyes: to see such a terrible thing!

MOTHER: His only virtue; for that alone he might have been loved.

FATHER: Loved? Isn't that another one of those dirty jokes? I know a dirty joke. Yes, yes, it's about a little boy who used to build aeroplanes alone in bed at night. Such a nice hobby for a little boy! Don't you think so? I mean stained sheets and all . . . I mean—even so—stained sheets . . . I MEAN GLUE ALL OVER HIS SHEETS! If he had a welding torch he might have built a real aeroplane, and flown from the window through the moonlight.

MOTHER: Like a stupid old fedora thrown from a window.

FATHER: But, Mother, I know a dirty joke. Let me tell you the dirty joke.

MOTHER: A dirty joke! Get out of here! A husband who was his father's stupid old fedora. A husband who ended up becoming his mother's old dress!

FATHER: That's not true! I admit to having been an old woman's stocking hanging at an old lady's ankle: she was trooping around a grocery store trying to impress the grocer with her varicosity. But, she kicked me off with a sudden desire to place her calloused walking thing in his face, that he might look down her leg to something more typical of her gender.

MOTHER: I never did such a thing! That's a dirty rotten filthy lie! Perhaps I stooped a little to pull my stocking up, a perfectly natural excuse to relieve his chronic curiosity about the true nature of my, my . . . *sitting organ*, which, with great sensitivity, he hid by talking to another customer.

FATHER: That's a dirty rotten filthy lie! He didn't say a word to me!

MOTHER: I suppose you didn't ask him to look at your aeroplane, or was it your knee?

FATHER: I do not take notice of such things. I was watching

a rather handsome young woman wearing a mustache, leading a dog on a chain.

MOTHER: *A handsome young woman wearing a mustache, leading a dog on a chain!* Who are you fooling?

[*Their son screams.*]

FATHER: Something's hurt, Mother.

MOTHER: Something is always complaining.

[*Their son screams again.*]

FATHER: Maybe it's the toilet. You know how lonely the toilet gets for the plumber.

MOTHER: *Who* gets lonely for the plumber? Well, call the plumber! Call the greengrocer, maybe he'll take you for the toilet and plug you up with a rutabaga.

FATHER: A rutabaga? You know that I prefer Swedish turnips. [*Going to the window and yelling*] Plumber, plumber, greengrocer, anyone, HELP!

MOTHER: Do you have to tell all the family secrets to the universe for our neighbors to hear?

FATHER [*from the window again*]: Neighbors, neighbors, do not listen while I tell the universe about our toilet!

[*Their son screams again.*]

MOTHER: Maybe it's the door.

FATHER: But, Mother, why should the door want to scream?

MOTHER: It's hungry. Things scream when they're hungry— probably hungry for a stranger; doors are always hungry for strangers.

FATHER: If the door's a mouth, I must be its tongue.

MOTHER: You're a silly old man who looks like an old woman's dress.

FATHER: No, no, Mother, I sometimes wear a fedora, as did my father, as did his, which shows people that I have love with a trunk in the attic; and the trunk gives birth to a *baby* old lady's dress. See? Now that makes sense. And maybe people say to the old lady's dress, [*in falsetto*] "My, you look just like your old trunk-loving daddy." See the sense of it? That's why you think I look like an old lady's dress. It's really the old lady's dress that looks like me.

MOTHER: Oh, do what you want in the attic, see if I care!

FATHER: But Mother, please listen!

MOTHER: I don't want to hear it!

FATHER: Yes, yes, but my shoe pinches my foot in a very suggestive way. Not to mention the easy chair holding me in its arms.

[*Their son screams again.*]

MOTHER: Something is very wrong, and you go on like a coquette.

FATHER: Wrong? . . . Is it that the walls want love with me? Will the house fall down if the walls lean toward my bed with desire?

MOTHER: I hate you!

[*Their son screams again.*]

FATHER: Why do things scream?

MOTHER: To flush our attention down the toilets of their desire.

[*They stiffen as though startled by something unseen by the audience. A small pause, and then they fall to the floor and are still.*]

PART TWO

[*The family is on the kitchen floor, all unconscious where they last fell.*]

[*After a few moments the son begins to make vague doglike movements, whining and yipping, as when dogs dream of running.*]

7

SON [*waking up*]: Coming awake, coming awake—Awake! When I snap my fingers you will be awake, you will remember nothing. [*He snaps his fingers, jerks his head, startled and confused.*]

[*He points at his own face as though separated from himself.*] Who are you? . . . Wait!

[*He goes to his mother lying on the floor, lifts her apron, and looks under it for a moment, shakes his head sadly and pulls it up over her face.*] Where I came from isn't there anymore.

[*She convulses.*]

[*He looks down toward the seat of his pants, pointing.*] Who are you? What are you? [*He cringes from his lower body.*]

[*He becomes still for a moment, and then looks upward, as though to Heaven.*] I'm the one down here . . . Heaven's nether flesh . . .

[*Now he goes to his unconscious father and looks up one of his pant legs.*] Oh my God! Father's knee.

[*His father convulses.*]

[*He goes to the kitchen table and takes a coffee cup and holds it out like a skull.*] . . . Cup, because a cup is shaped like a cup, little skull of the midnight coffee-brain . . . Identity being more in shape than essence . . . The appearance of things. [*Noticing his own shadow*] . . . If one is nothing, one is still an object shaped like a person . . . The shadow of someone. [*He falls into his own shadow, and is still.*]

PART THREE

[*Everyone is on the floor where they were at the end of Part Two.*]

[*The father and mother begin to stir.*]

MOTHER (*yawning and pointing to her son*): Something's wrong with the floor.

FATHER (*tilting his head*): Perhaps it's a distant mountain.

MOTHER: How could a distant mountain get in our kitchen?!

FATHER: Through the window?

MOTHER: Through the window?!

FATHER: Well I don't know what it is. Maybe it's a valley disguised as a mountain.

MOTHER: Maybe it isn't a mountain or a valley; something else . . . Exhibit A.

FATHER: No, no, perhaps, perhaps it's something not too near us, yet, yet, yet, yet, not that far away as to be said to be *that* far away . . . Secluded and private, with a lovely view, but convenient for shopping, the greengrocer's, the plumber . . .

MOTHER: Stop it, stop it, stop it!

FATHER: But, but, but, couldn't we carry on our lives without noticing it?

MOTHER: Go to it, Father, find out what it is. Ask it!

FATHER: Oh no, Mother—please!

MOTHER: Ask it!

FATHER [*approaching his son with shrinking*]: Who . . . who are you, sir?—No, don't answer, that would be too fearful. Let me take it for granted that you are either God, or some person of awesome power. We and our kitchen are completely at your disposal.

[*There is no answer.*]

MOTHER: Kick it, Father.

FATHER: It might bite.

MOTHER: What is it?

FATHER [*edging closer*]: It might be one of us.

MOTHER: We are in our own selves!

FATHER [*facing away from his wife*]: Where are you, Mother?

MOTHER: In *this* old woman.

9

FATHER: What old woman?

MOTHER: Your wife, that pretty young thing!

FATHER [*looking upward*]: Help me.

MOTHER: What is it, Father?

FATHER: I think it's someone faraway, asleep, who has managed by some strange proximity to be in our kitchen.

MOTHER: If it's mobile, tell it to go. I will not have it in my kitchen.

FATHER: Oh, Mother, I don't know what it is . . . Hmmm, it does seem to have legs. But they may only be phony ones . . . Hmmm, it seems to have a shadow. But I can't tell whether it's a drawing with its shadow drawn in, or a hole in the floor.

MOTHER: Well, walk on it!

FATHER: But it could be a hole in the floor!

MOTHER: Experiment!

FATHER: You mean if it's a mountain, climb it and crash through the ceiling? If it's a hole fall down into the cellar? No! No! No!

MOTHER: Oh, God! Author of goodness, author of cruelty . . .

FATHER: Let's not fool with this thing anymore!

MOTHER: Let's not do anything anymore.

FATHER: We'll just wait.

MOTHER: For what?

FATHER: For the *external* to make itself known.

MOTHER [*bitterly*]: Oh no, I've been hidden all my life, let the *external* hide itself for a while.

FATHER: My dear wife, and mother of my only child, you are the *external*. I am the *internal*—all my life—the surpressed explosion.

MOTHER: You are nothing!

FATHER: I have a shadow, which allows that I am something shaped like a person, mounted on legs.

MOTHER: I don't care for your legs.

FATHER: The world is perfectly willing to mind its own business while someone is dying under his fedora.

MOTHER: Your fedora can be used as a spittoon.

FATHER: Wife, wife, love my hairy belly!

MOTHER [*inspired*]: In the springtime . . .

FATHER: Yes?

MOTHER: In the time of pubescence . . . The green wood . . . Birds fluting the air.

FATHER: . . . From the high hill, the sea as blue as Hokusai said it was.

MOTHER: The maiden, half girl, half woman. Oh, how I loved myself then!

FATHER: I adore you!

MOTHER: No, no, you are not there to adore.

FATHER: Pretend.

MOTHER: No, no, you'll spoil it.

FATHER: No, no, Mother, let me be in it too.

MOTHER: No, no, you're home masturbating over pictures of your father.

FATHER: . . . How I ruined my mind visualizing Father wearing his fedora in strange landscapes.

MOTHER: Oh please, is there no *end* to the end?

FATHER: It goes on and on. The beginning is always with us. Let us go to the green wood.

MOTHER: No! It is over, thank God!

FATHER: Never to be again?

11

MOTHER: Over! Over! Over!

FATHER: As is this time?

MOTHER: As is any time seen far from itself.

FATHER: Ah, mother, the romance of it!

MOTHER [*sobbing*]: But it's always *now*.

FATHER: Soon to be *then*.

MOTHER: To get past this time, to be safe in the future.

FATHER: But, Mother, this *is* the future.

MOTHER: No, no, this is *right now!*

FATHER: But it's also the future of some past unhappiness.

MOTHER: And see how it turned out?

FATHER: It's still turning out.

MOTHER: Oh, Father, will it never stop?

FATHER: Not as long as it doesn't.

MOTHER: *What* doesn't?

FATHER: I forget, and that's how it sneaks up on you.

MOTHER: What sneaks up on us?!

FATHER: I forget . . . And again, that's how it keeps sneaking up on us.

MOTHER: Oh, father, what are we doing here?

FATHER: Didn't we come to kill something?

MOTHER: Then why all this delay?

FATHER: Because to *be* is most of the battle.

MOTHER: And now that we *are?*

FATHER: If we *are*, then we're ready to branch out.

MOTHER: Oh, Father!

FATHER [*pointing to the son*]: As to that . . .

MOTHER: —Unavoidably . . .

FATHER: —Exactly, what?

MOTHER: That which was become of us in our coitus.

FATHER: Which was, besides the huffing and puffing? . . .

MOTHER: —So to speak . . .

FATHER: —So to speak *what?*

MOTHER: Something that's been with us.

FATHER: —Why with us?

MOTHER: Oh, because it manages, by some strange proximity, to be on our kitchen floor, where it has lain thirty or forty years. Because I'm so sick of it!—Of you!—This kitchen!

FATHER: Was it the son we had not loved?

MOTHER: It was something!

FATHER: Was it the son?!

MOTHER: Do I know? It was someone who often came as a baby.

FATHER: A baby?

MOTHER: You know, something that cries through the noise of the birds at sunset.

FATHER: At sunset?

MOTHER: Yes, yes, the closing of the day!

FATHER: What cries?

MOTHER: The baby!

FATHER: Why?

MOTHER: Out of pity for itself, that it should stir again.

FATHER: What stirs?

MOTHER: Life out of the safety of un-being.

FATHER: And so it cries? But, doesn't it also scream?

13

MOTHER: Yes, yes, because its comfort is lost forever.

FATHER: Who is this baby?

MOTHER: It's the one I was talking about. Our son!

FATHER: And all this talk is about *him?*

MOTHER: Do you not remember how he came out of my body?

FATHER: You mean that man who hangs around here came out of your body?

MOTHER: Of course. Don't you remember?

FATHER: I only remember your going into a big building and coming out of it with a miniature person who kept weeping.— And yes, screaming!

MOTHER: That person is your son.

FATHER: I don't like it. Something's very wrong with a universe that treats human affairs so casually. You'd better go back to the big building.

MOTHER: That was years ago, I don't remember the address.

FATHER: Then we are in trouble.

MOTHER: Why?

FATHER: Because it's our own son we do not love.

MOTHER: There's also you.

FATHER: And you! [*He sticks his tongue out at her.*]

[*They stiffen and fall to the floor, and are still.*]

PART FOUR

[*As before, all are on the floor where they fell previously. The father and mother moan as they come awake. Their son is still, but his mouth is open as if formed to scream. As the mother and father talk they remain on the floor.*]

14

MOTHER [*noticing her husband*]: Who are you?

FATHER: I must presume to be whoever I was. To be is half the battle . . . By the way, Miss, who are you?

MOTHER: That's hardly your affair.

FATHER: Affair?—That's it, you're the greengrocer's wife, and we're having an affair . . . By the way, where's your mustache?

MOTHER: You're not the one, I've never seen you before in my life—unless . . . unless you're my husband?

FATHER: I'm not married to an old lady! I would have married my own mother if it came to that. Are you trying to say that you are more desirable than my own mother?!

MOTHER: You old fool, you're an old woman yourself, and that thing over there is your son.

FATHER [*thinking she has mistaken him for his son*]: I am not!

MOTHER: No, no, that thing over there with its mouth open.

FATHER [*mistaking his wife for himself*]: Then you must be the *daddy* . . .

MOTHER: No, no, you're the daddy—the *father!* It's your fault!

FATHER: Yes, that's how it was: I had been reclining on a floor so as to look up the leg of some chair. And then you came in; and thinking that I was some kind of an animal rug you stood on me. Yes, you thought, what a luxurious rug, as you dug your shoes into me. And thinking that I was being properly paid for previous sins I made no effort to correct your cruelty. But, there is a kind of joy even in the punitive. As you perched on my face, digging your heels into my forehead, one of my eyes, only partially covered under your instep, looked up your leg and saw how the woman is different from the chair. Oh, the rose in scent!—The glands most liquid!

MOTHER: Enough! You were like some old woman's dress that blew off a clothesline through my bedroom window one night. You kept insisting, "Let me show you how I am a man!" I said,

15

"Damn you! Whatever you are, let me sleep!" You reminded me of an old woman's dress, some old thing belonging to Mother . . .

FATHER: Who am I? Am I *you* talking to me? Why am I on the floor? Did I fall?—From where? What is all this? I must get out of here! [*He gets up.*]

MOTHER: Sure, the trunk in the attic, the greengrocer . . . But, your son . . .

FATHER: My son?!

MOTHER: Your son!

FATHER: But, I'm a child myself, you cannot expect me to father another child.

MOTHER: Down to the grocer, and up his ass!

FATHER: But, I'm a child, myself!

MOTHER: You're a terrible old rag that needs a woman to give it shape.

FATHER: How dare you say that I require female company!

MOTHER: Come and do love with me. [*She holds out her arms.*]

FATHER: No, no, once was enough!

MOTHER: Once *what?*

FATHER [*pointing to his son*]: You don't expect me to father that thing again?

MOTHER: No, no, this time for love.

FATHER [*to himself*]: Why am I thinking of dirty jokes? I must go to the greengrocer's—ah, there's a place!

MOTHER: For what?

FATHER: The journey.

MOTHER: The anticipation?

FATHER: Something or other.

16

MOTHER: The woman with the mustache?

FATHER: Yes, yes, damn you! The woman with the mustache!

MOTHER: Who is really a man?

FATHER: If it turns out that way.

MOTHER: But it never happens, does it, Father?

FATHER: Of course not, that would be too shameful.

MOTHER [*pointing to her son*]: Him.

FATHER: I'm on my way to the greengrocer's, and I don't want anything to do with *that;* that's a decision I'm not ready to make.

MOTHER: But suppose it doesn't love us anymore?

FATHER: Suppose it never did?

MOTHER: Get out of here, you have made me unhappy.

[*He sticks his tongue out at her, goes for the door, falls, and is still.*]

[*The son rises and staggers about moaning.*]

MOTHER [*facing away from her son, unaware that it is he*]: The voice of God?

SON: Mother?

MOTHER: To become incarnate again?

SON [*screaming*]: Mother!

MOTHER: Yes, yes, I can't say no!

SON: I'm hungry!

MOTHER: *Anything*, my God—my breasts, my cupboard!

SON [*screaming*]: I'm hungry!

MOTHER: Come to me, or show Yourself that I might come to You.

SON: Where are you?

17

MOTHER: Has God become blind in His old age?

SON [*screaming*]: Mother, Mother, Mother!

MOTHER: Please, You frighten me. Show me how I might serve You.

SON: Do you love me?

MOTHER [*with a sudden realization that the voice is her son's*]: *You!*

SON: Do you love me?

MOTHER: I do not love.

SON: Please love me.

MOTHER: How can I love *you?*

SON: Feed me. Feed me. Feed me.

MOTHER: I do not like to feed you.

SON: Feed me!

MOTHER: Lick the dirt from the floor.

SON: Feed me!

MOTHER: I'll kill you!

SON: Why?

MOTHER: Because you interrupt me!

SON: From what?

MOTHER: Myself.

SON: What are you doing that you cannot feed me?

MOTHER: I'm trying not to think of anything.

SON: But I'm hungry.

MOTHER: Go to the cupboard! Die! Stop interrupting me!

SON: I need you.

MOTHER: For what?

SON: To feed me.

MOTHER: Why?

SON: Because I need you to love me.

MOTHER: I do not love you! I will not feed you!

[*They both fall to the floor, and are still.*]

PART FIVE

[*They are all on the floor, unconscious. After a few moments the son begins to stir.*]

SON: Coming awake . . . Coming awake . . . When I snap my fingers you will be awake—you will remember nothing. [*He snaps his fingers, and jerks his head as though suddenly awake. A small pause, and then pointing at his own face he asks:*] Who are you? [*Going to his mother and lifting her apron*] Nope. [*He pulls the apron up over her face; she convulses. Now he goes to the kitchen table and raps on it.*] Do I hear my twin sister? [*He goes to the door, steps out, and returns wearing a very yellow wig. He speaks his twin sister's lines in falsetto.*]

TWIN SISTER [*brightly, looking at her parents on the floor*]: Hello Mom and Dad, I've been in the world. I've just come off the street. I was just passing by like anyone. Why, I might have been anyone, just . . . anyone . . . really, just anyone passing by. But, suddenly I was your daughter . . . In the world I'm a woman who runs a school where aeroplanes are taught to be tender. [*Trivial laughter*]—Just as tender as they can be.

SON [*he runs to the door and puts his head out, shouting*]: I'm hungry, feed me!

TWIN SISTER [*returning*]:—A school to teach aeroplanes to be tender—after I lost my mind. Yes, I lost my mind while dressing one day: Thinking it was only a cuff button that had rolled under the dresser. It was my mind, I had become quite insane. [*Trivial laughter*] I remember an aeroplane flying by and winking at me. That's nice, I screamed! But, I couldn't think anymore, I'd have to remember how I used to do things.

SON [*taking the wig off*]: I'm hungry!

TWIN SISTER [*putting the wig on*]: . . . How I used to do things: I used to fall down the stairs because it saved me the effort of walking down the stairs.

SON [*taking the wig off*]: Please!

TWIN SISTER [*putting the wig on*]: I used to stay unconscious at the bottom of the stairs for several hours, which . . . which saved me the effort of having to climb back up to my bedroom to sleep. Clever, huh? [*Trivial laughter*]

SON [*taking the wig off*]: Hungry!

TWIN SISTER [*putting the wig on*]: . . . I stood in the yard and taught aeroplanes to be tender. As they flew over I screamed BE TENDER! And they would fly away just as tenderly . . . being tender wherever they went.

SON [*taking the wig off*]: But I must eat!

TWIN SISTER [*putting the wig on*]: Then it was dinner time. I went to the kitchen to see if the kitchen had cooked anything. —Oh no, the kitchen is always too busy entertaining flies. I was able to solve most of the problems of the world by setting fire to the house. And I was able to find cooked things; a feather pillow, which I decided was a chicken . . . if I shut my eyes.

SON [*taking the wig off*]: No more, no more, please, I'm hungry!

TWIN SISTER [*putting the wig on*]: Through my enterprise [*Trivial laughter*] I was able to save myself the effort of cleaning the house. Such a dirty house! A dirty rotten filthy house! —which made no effort to keep its hair combed. I asked the house, will you please serve my breakfast in bed? Will you please run my bath?—NO!—and the walls standing around like hoodlums in their corners.

SON [*taking the wig off*]: THE STORY'S TOO LONG!

TWIN SISTER [*putting the wig on*]: From disorder into greater disorder . . . I was forced to scream from the window, which wasn't unpleasant, quite a nice hobby; becoming even more important than teaching aeroplanes to be tender. Surely I would spread tenderness, but first I would SCREAM! I needed only a window and a mouth. I had a window, so I felt around my face for a mouth. Yes, yes, I have a mouth, I screamed!—My mouth is SCREAMING! . . . But then I saw a vase, and its mouth was open, too. Could it be screaming? If it is, I thought, I shall be very envious, which is rather negative, wouldn't you say? I said to the vase, if it is you who are screaming, please do not scream. But the vase continued to scream until I became very envious. And so I was forced to smash it.

SON [*taking the wig off*]: It's too long.

TWIN SISTER [*putting the wig on*]: But the screaming didn't stop, and I noticed an open door: Please, door, do not scream, because I am becoming very envious. But the door continued to scream. Must I clear the whole world of screaming things before I can scream? And now the toilet began to scream . . . It was a time of much screaming.

[*He takes the wig off and screams.*]

TWIN SISTER [*putting the wig on*]: I decided that I would be forced to fall out of the window because I have not learned how to fly. I said to myself, you must fall out of the window because you have not learned how to fly. I said, okay, if that's the way you want it—[*Throwing the wig into the air and falling on the floor*]—I fell out of the window. [*Putting the wig on*] And as I was falling an aeroplane passed, and I screamed, BE TENDER! —as tender as you cannnnnnnn . . .

SON [*taking the wig off*]: Be tender!

TWIN SISTER [*putting the wig on*]: When I came awake after that rather interesting experience, all the screaming had died. I asked the stairs to carry me up to my room in their banister arms. They refused, and so I dragged myself up by the hair of somebody's head to my room.

SON [*taking the wig off, sobbing*]: Mother, I'm hungry!

TWIN SISTER [*putting on the wig*]: And then, while dressing one day, my mind rolled under the dresser. I thought it was a cuff button. But then I realized I couldn't possibly button my cuffs with my mind . . . Too late, too late, I noticed that I had become quite insane, I had lost my mind. And now an aeroplane winks at me. That's nice!—A good start toward the way I have not yet determined—something—yet, toward what thing? My cuff button begins to think.

SON [*taking the wig off*]: Go away!

TWIN SISTER [*putting on the wig; teasingly*]: I'm Father's favorite. [*She sticks her tongue out.*]

[*He takes the wig off and makes a face.*]

[*She puts the wig on and makes a face.*]

[*He takes the wig off and makes a face.*]

[*She puts the wig on and makes a face.*]

[*He takes the wig off and makes a face.*]

[*She puts the wig on and makes a hideous face.*]

SON [*still wearing the wig, he starts punching himself on his shoulders and chest*]: You get out of here! Get out! Get out! [*He punches and beats his twin sister out of the door. He re-enters, minus the wig, and looks at the audience with great sadness, and says:*] Mother, I'm hungry.

[*He falls to the floor, and is still.*]

PART SIX

[*They are all on the floor unconscious. But, now the father is wearing the yellow wig, and the mother is wearing a mustache; the son is wearing his mother's apron.*]

[*The father and mother convulse and moan, slowly returning to consciousness.*]

FATHER: Oh God . . . Because comfort is lost forever . . .

MOTHER: What stirs?

FATHER: It's lost, forever.

MOTHER: Am I loved?

FATHER: Was anything ever loved?

MOTHER [*suddenly aware*]: And just who are you?

FATHER: I've never seen either one of us in my life—unless you're my husband?

MOTHER: Am I married to an old woman? No, no, impossible, I would have married my own mother if it had come to that!

FATHER: Admit it, you're curious about my aeroplane.

[*The son suddenly sits up, his mouth wide as though to scream. He pulls his apron up, looks under it for a moment, screams, and falls back pulling the apron over his face.*]

MOTHER [*mistaking her son for herself, and herself for her husband*]: My wife is having a baby!

FATHER: Not that again!

MOTHER: A son.

FATHER: Something else.

MOTHER: Thirty or forty years . . . Exhibit A.

FATHER: Criminally assaulting my view.

MOTHER: For that easily loved.

FATHER: The journey!

MOTHER: The anticipation. [*Holding her arms out to him*] The woman with the mustache?

FATHER [*falling into her arms*]: Yes, yes, damn you!—the woman with the mustache . . .[*Sobbing*] Did we ever love anything?

MOTHER: Didn't we, once in a while, Father?

FATHER: I remember earlier there was that lovely feeling that we would soon love something.

MOTHER: But something had to love us first, didn't it, Father?

FATHER: A dog licked my hand once. Yes, a rather handsome young woman wearing a mustache, had a dog on a chain. The dog had broken loose.

MOTHER: What a lovely dog. I love that dog.

FATHER: Why do you love that dog and not your husband?

MOTHER: That is a lovely dog, and its tail wags.

FATHER: I was forced to beat the dog, because I knew it was just a matter of time before he fastened his jaws to my throat.

MOTHER: Did you hurt the nice dog, Father?

FATHER: The dog had secret plans to open my throat; perhaps out of curiosity—or was it hunger? Perhaps it was just another form of parental cruelty.

MOTHER: Did you hurt the nice dog, Father?

FATHER: And I do not like people who like animals instead of people!

MOTHER: But, that was a nice dog, Father, that was a good friend.

FATHER: It was an enemy disguised as a friendly dog. But soon he was yelping and running away from me. And I was able that very night to tell Mother and Father that I hated them. Uncle George said, "That's not nice." I said, "*Uncle George, will you please keep out of this!*"

MOTHER: Did you ever see that nice dog again?

FATHER: Yes. The next time I saw it, it growled and chased me home.

MOTHER: You didn't hurt it again, did you?

FATHER: No, no, it chased me home. And when I got home I said to Mother and Father, "I love you." And Uncle George said, "Now that's the way I like to hear my nephew talk." And I said, "*Uncle George, will you PLEASE keep out of this!*"

MOTHER: So what did the dog do?

FATHER: Will you stop annoying me about that dog—it lifted its leg and pissed!

MOTHER: And then what happened?

FATHER: It met another dog and mated with it; but discovering that its partner was male, blushed.

MOTHER: Oh Father, you mean he was queer?

FATHER: No—I said he *blushed*—he made a mistake. He was really queer for my throat.

MOTHER: Did we ever love anything?

FATHER: It's this, Mother, everyone wishes he were loved, but no one will love anything.

MOTHER: But, Father, can't they pretend?

FATHER: It's too much bother.

MOTHER: What else have they to do?

FATHER: Well, why doesn't our son love us?

MOTHERS He's trying to get even with us for not loving him.

FATHER: He was always spiteful.

MOTHER: I try to exnore him.

FATHER: He's trying to break our hearts. He wants to say, *"Ha, ha, fooled you, you love me, but I don't love you!"*

MOTHER: Why does he want to hurt us, Father?

FATHER: Why? . . . Because he's no different from those that hurt him.

MOTHER: The copycat!—and who hurt him anyway?

FATHER: He thinks we did.

MOTHER: What did we do to him?

FATHER: I think he wanted us to love and cuddle him.

MOTHER: I wouldn't do that for my own child!

FATHER: But, Mother, he *is* your own child.

MOTHER: So what, I just said I wouldn't do it for my own child.

FATHER: So he's out to ruin us by denying us the love he owes us.

MOTHER: What can we do to protect ourselves against this cruel denial?

FATHER: We must carry on as if we didn't care. It's easy, I just pretend he's my mother, and say to him, "*Mother, I don't love you either!*" He just looks at me . . . Did we ever teach him to talk?

MOTHER: I never taught him anything. I thought, if you can get yourself born you can teach yourself to talk . . . He may've picked it up from the radio.

FATHER: I wonder sometimes if we shouldn't just kill him?

MOTHER: I would love to knock his head in. Did you ever notice how much he looks like my father?

FATHER: I would love to knock your father's head in.

MOTHER: I would love to knock everybody's head in!—Oh, if only I could murder the whole world!

FATHER: Please, Mother, not the whole world, I'm still in it.

MOTHER: Oh, Father—not murder the world, I'd just like to squeeze it a little.

FATHER: Your mind wanders.

MOTHER: My mind can go anywhere it pleases.

FATHER: I do not like your mind, nor do I like your body.

MOTHER: Have I ever liked *you?*

FATHER: I'm not asking you to like me.

MOTHER: That's good, because I don't.

FATHER: That's what I mean about you.

MOTHER: Ho ho, you can't make me like you!

FATHER: See how you're way off the subject?

MOTHER: Well, damn you, what is the subject?!

FATHER: Don't you remember?

MOTHER: Remember? Remember *what?* What have I ever known worth remembering?

FATHER: Mother, sometimes I would love to have your neck in my hands, and squeeze all the rottenness out of the world.

MOTHERS [*with exquisite hatred*]: Ooo, I wish you'd try it.

FATHER: Damn you! Damn you!

MOTHER: Oh damn yourself! [*She sticks her tongue out at him.*]

FATHER: Don't you—[*Sobbing*]—remember?

MOTHER: Remember what?—Father's Day?!

FATHER [*on the floor kicking and sobbing*]: No, no, no, no, no!

MOTHER: What? You fool.

FATHER: Our son!

MOTHER: Well, what about him?

FATHER: You just want me to say it.

MOTHER: Say *what?*

FATHER: That we're going to . . . knock-your-father's-head-in!

MOTHER: Well? . . .

FATHER [*raging*]: No, no, no, that's not it!

MOTHER: Well, what is it?!

FATHER: That we're going to . . . knock-your-father's-head-in!

MOTHER: Well, knock his head in, see if I care!

FATHER: No, no, not him!

27

MOTHER: Then, who?

FATHER [*screaming*]: YOUR FATHER!

MOTHER: I'm growing out of patience with you.

FATHER: I'LL KILL GOD!

MOTHER: Then do it.

FATHER: I'll kill that homosexual dog!

MOTHER: Kill anything you damn well please!

FATHER [*on the floor screaming and kicking*]: I'll kill you! I'll turn you to worms! I'll kill you! I'll kill your son! I'll kill him! I'll kill him!

MOTHER: Then kill him!

FATHER [*looking at their son*]: . . . That's *it*, I'll kill him.

MOTHER: Let me help.

FATHER [*to her*]: Help me.

MOTHER: I said I'd help.

FATHER: Then do it!

MOTHER: Do it? I said I'd *help* you.

FATHER [*he approaches his son crouched in a comic boxer's stance, using silly dancelike footwork*]: Stand up and fight like a man!

SON [*suddenly awake, screaming*]: Don't, don't, don't!

FATHER: Come on, I ain't afraid of you!

SON [*he gets up shrinkingly, his hands over his face*]: Don't, don't!

FATHER [*dancing around his son without landing a blow*]: Come on, Mother, help me, he's tougher than I thought.

[*The son continues to hide his face, shrinking with fear.*]

[*Now the mother joins her husband in the same comic boxer's dance around her son. At this time no blows have been landed.*]

28

FATHER: He's pretty good!

MOTHER: S'got a nice left!

[*The son is crying rather loudly and clutching his groin as he wets on himself.*]

[*Now the mother and father begin to land blows on him, beating him to the ground.*]

SON [*screaming*]: Don't, don't, don't!

[*The parents are breathing with a sexual intensity. When they finish their son is bloodied and crumpled on the floor.*]

MOTHER: Sonofabitch, didn't want to die!

FATHER: Bastard!

PART SEVEN

[*The son is on the floor where he last fell at the hands of his parents. He is without any signs of the previous violence, the blood is gone and his pants are dry. He is wearing a mustache and he has an artificial dog on a chain.*

[*He gets up, yawns and stretches, as though after a good sleep. And then he casually strolls to the front of the stage and looks into the audience thoughtfully, as though expecting someone.*

[*After a short time the door bursts open and two policemen rush in. They are his parents, fully uniformed and carrying nightsticks. The mother-policeman is wearing her apron over her uniform. The father-policeman is wearing the yellow wig.*]

MOTHER: Where is the parricide?!

FATHER: What parricide?

MOTHER: Exhibit A., wearing a mustache, with a dog on a chain. The one who criminally assaulted someone's view.

FATHER: —And could easily be loved for that! Oh, what a terrible weapon!

MOTHER: All that blood! Used an aeroplane, I understand.

FATHER: Did you see all that glue? I say he's a brat!

MOTHER: A brat?—Did you see what he did to his parents?

FATHER: Glue all over his sheets, making aeroplanes alone in bed at night. Just think what he might have done with a welding torch!

MOTHER [*to her son*]: Excuse me, sir, have you seen the parricide? [*Noticing his dog*]—Oh, what a lovely dog.

SON: The *who*-cide?

MOTHER: Exhibit A., someone who often came as a baby.

SON: A baby?

MOTHER: You know, something that cries through the noise of the birds at sunset.

SON: At sunset?

MOTHER: Yes, yes—the closing of the day!

SON: It cries?

MOTHER: The parricide!—the one wearing a mustache!

SON: Why?

MOTHER: Out of pity for itself, that it should stir again.

SON: What stirs?

MOTHER: The parricide!—Exhibit A.!

FATHER: The one who criminally assaults someone's view, and could easily be loved for that!

SON: And who is the *baby?*

MOTHER: The parricide! The one I've been talking about— thirty or forty years—Exhibit A.!

SON [*beginning to sob*]: I'm hungry.

FATHER [*to his wife*]: The witness is hungry.

MOTHER: So is parricide, let's be careful. [*To her son*] You mean you're *hungry*? . . .

SON [*sobbing*]: I'm hungry.

MOTHER [*taking a notebook out and writing in it*]: . . . First . . . requirement . . . of . . . love . . .

FATHER: We're not here to have love.

MOTHER [*writing*]: . . . Not . . . here . . . for . . . love . . . [*Raising her voice*] We were never here for love!

FATHER: But, can't we pretend? I know a dirty joke: There was once this tender aeroplane . . .

MOTHER: It's too much bother!

FATHER: But, what else is there to do?

MOTHER [*holding her arms out*]: Okay, come and do love then.

FATHER: Do I dare?

MOTHER: Of course, my sweet old boy, my poor old sweety.

FATHER: You love me?

MOTHER: Please don't ask that.

FATHER: May I kiss you?

MOTHER: You may kiss my badge.

FATHER [*kissing her badge with much passion*]: Oh my darling!

MOTHER: There, there, old boy, love-starved old sweety.

FATHER: I've been so alone, so alone . . .

MOTHER: Poor old boy, my poor old boy . . .

[*He wanders out of the embrace dazed, groping like a blind man, until he finds a chair.*]

FATHER [*to the chair*]: Oh, please, let us be foul! [*He feels under the seat of the chair obscenely as he kisses it.*] You are

31

more lovely—I adore you! You are my potency! [*He tips the chair over and goes down on the floor with it.*] You are the most beautiful, the most, the most . . . [*He loses contact with the chair and rolls over helplessly with groping hands.*] Oh God, God—unhappy—alone!

[*His wife begins to beat him with her nightstick.*]

FATHER: Kisses! Kisses!

MOTHER: The world is full of pain.

FATHER: And cruel kisses!

MOTHER: Oh, it's too sad.

[*He clings to his wife's feet, and the son kneels before her.*]

MOTHER: Oh, ganging up, huh?

SON [*lifting his mother's apron and looking under it*]: Where I came from is policeman's pants. All comfort is lost; nor is there the food that consoles. [*He buries his face in the apron and weeps.*]

MOTHER [*to the audience, as though concluding a lecture*]: Compassion? Of course. Toward something else? Ritual? Perhaps.

[*Both the father and the son are sobbing and weeping loudly.*]

MOTHER: Uplifting? Perhaps.

[*The father and the son continue their sobbing and weeping.*]

MOTHER [*as if inviting the audience, swaying, almost dancing*]: Should we dance? Shall we?

[*With a frightened expression on her face she falls to the floor. On their backs they all lie separated from each other, mouths open, eyes blank and staring, hands clutching out, frozen.*]

CURTAIN

The Crawlers

The Crawlers

This is an amusement about a father, a daughter, and her suitor. The father, a middle-aged businessman, attempts to arrange a marriage for his daughter. She is a fat woman in her forties, habituated to shapeless housecoats; her hair is set in pin curls, or any other unfortunate decoration. She is problemed with sexual loneliness, or, as it is often called, romantic longing. In remedy of the chronic irritation the father has invited a younger man from his office. This man is in his thirties, and is the type who wears cheap suits, complemented with equally tasteless ties.

[*The father and daughter are sitting in the living room. He is reading a newspaper. She entertains herself, making faces and odd gestures, with a kind of infantile self-centeredness. Every so often he looks around his newspaper at her with pained, angry annoyance.*]

FATHER [*scrutinizing his daughter*]: There's enough of you to make two daughters; both of them horribly fat women.

DAUGHTER [*as though unaware of him*]: Goo goo, da da.

FATHER: Stop that hideous baby talk! You're not at all cute. [*Softening*] Please, you must try to hide your gluttony with a quiet dignity.

DAUGHTER [*exaggerated haughtiness*]: Like this, Daddy dear?

FATHER [*shaking his head with exasperation*]: A kind of wistful reserve; exaggerated behavior only points to your exaggerated bulk. I've invited a young man from the office to meet you tonight.

DAUGHTER [*with great happiness*]: Oh, Daddy!

FATHER: Even for all your gluttony, my daughter, disadvantage that it is, you are blessed with a rich father. Young men are prisoners in their desire to be rich. They are in particular awe of my office chair, with all its squeaks and grunts, the torn leather, the splintered wood; which, in symbol, one must admit, is like a throne.

DAUGHTER: Oh, Daddy, you bore me with your silly old chair. I want to talk about romance, not your dumb old business.

FATHER: You'd better be glad I have a *dumb old business,* so I can afford to buy you a husband. Yes, I'm buying you a husband! I'm making an utter stranger an heir so you'll have reason to go to bed, instead of sitting around all night making baby sounds.

DAUGHTER: Is he pretty?

FATHER: Pretty? How do I know? Am I a homosexual? I don't look at men that way. One might say he looks *healthy*.

DAUGHTER: Is he awful nice?

FATHER: Unfortunately he's one of those shoe-kissers. A terrible habit. One never knows how far up the leg his intentions go. Yet, who wouldn't come gladly to my feet? Is my business not almost an empire? Ah, but there is something so secondhand about him, a used floor model; damaged merchandise that should be sent back to the factory; in this case, back to his mother, either for re-use of the parts, or total repair. But this is no longer a buyer's market. [*Looking appraisingly at his daughter*] My God, I don't envy the poor man.

DAUGHTER: Do you think he'll come to my feet?

FATHER: I said he was a shoe-kisser. Shoe-kissers usually have a good nose for wealth. He'll probably begin the evening at my shoes. Then, when I tell him all that is mine will be yours, blah

blah, he'll likely find your shoes just as kissable. [*Noticing her sneakers*] I do wish you wouldn't wear those sneakers, they smell.

DAUGHTER: Oh, I wish he would just kiss me directly on my epidermis.

FATHER: Epidermis?! Where did you ever learn such a terrible word?

DAUGHTER: Maybe I should sit upside down on my chair, with my feet in the air, and my face hanging down on the floor, so he'll think my lips are feet.

FATHER: I suppose with your *epidermis* showing, so he'll not only think you fat, but *bearded!* Oh my dear, just be patient, if everything works out properly there'll not be a place on you he'll not kiss. But don't frighten him away with those odd postures. Your heft only points to itself when you start acting oddly.

DAUGHTER: Da da, goo goo.

FATHER: Are you starting to talk baby talk again?

DAUGHTER: I really think I ought to talk baby talk, it makes me seem cute.

FATHER: You are anything but cute!

DAUGHTER [*blinking eyes and taking various "cute" poses*]: Da da da da.

FATHER: Goddamn you! Goddamn you!

DAUGHTER: Goo goo [*Hiccup*] da da[*Hiccup*].

FATHER: Dirty slob, dirty fat slob!

DAUGHTER: Maybe I should put on a baby bonnet, and a lace bib?

FATHER: You're an aging fat woman. Why do you want to pretend to be an infant? You look like a drooling imbecile.

DAUGHTER: Daddy, look at this. [*She wags her tongue out of her mouth, her eyes blinking, and her limbs jerking with the useless motions of an infant.*] Da da, goo goo.

FATHER: No, no, no! It's hideous! Why do you refuse to be dignified?

DAUGHTER: Look at this, Daddy. [*She wags her head, and crosses her eyes in a monstrous imitation of an infant.*]

FATHER: If you don't stop I'll punch you in the face! I'll kick you in your stomach, you bitch, you dirty fat bitch!

DAUGHTER [*starting to cry*]: Why do you want to hurt me, just when I'm trying to make myself attractive? You don't know how lonely I've been. Men like baby dolls who wear diapers.

FATHER: Yes, cute young women with pert young bodies, wearing brassieres.

DAUGHTER [*supporting her breasts in her hands*]: What's wrong with these?

FATHER: Don't do that!

DAUGHTER [*rubbing her thighs*]: Plenty of everything.

FATHER: Too much of everything is more like it.

DAUGHTER: Da da. [*with sudden excitement*] Maybe I should wear a diaper?

FATHER: I'm warning you, you're going to get a punch right in the stomach.

DAUGHTER [*with a tough voice*]: Are you kidding, I could break you in half.

FATHER: Okay, you asked for it. [*He lunges and punches her in her stomach.*]

DAUGHTER [*holding her stomach*]: You dirty sonofabitch.

FATHER [*punching her in the jaw*]: Wow, that feels good!

[*She falls to the floor unconscious.*]

[*The father is unhappily aware that the man he has invited to meet his daughter is due any moment now, and she is on the floor unconscious. He is panting and pacing; each time he passes his daughter on the floor, he nudges her with his foot. After a few moments a scratching, or mild tapping is heard at the door. He gives his daughter a final and desperate nudge with his shoe as he answers the door. It is the man he has invited, a nervous and awkward person who keeps looking over his shoulder as if expecting to be followed. He blinks and moves his hands oddly.*]

FATHER [*exaggerated cheerfulness*]: Come in, come in. Have a seat. Let me get you a drink.

[*The man opens his mouth at the father, as though somehow adjusting his face.*]

FATHER [*ignoring the strange behavior and pouring a drink*]: I'd like you to meet my daughter. [*He nudges her with his foot.*]

[*The man sits on the couch with his hands folded; his eyes move foolishly about as he is handed his drink.*]

FATHER: Now, sir, no use beating around the bush, my daughter will be a very rich woman someday, and, well, you have eyes; it would be foolish of me to attempt to hide the fact that she is rather unattractive, fortyish, and overweight.

MAN: Yippee, I'm gonna be rich! I'm gonna be rich!

FATHER: You might pretend to feel something for my daughter. You do like women, don't you?

MAN: What? Who?

FATHER: You do have some of the manly feelings for a woman?

MAN: I'm going to be rich; then I shall not have to deal with scum like you.

FATHER: Who do you think you're talking to?!

39

MAN: I heard that someplace.

FATHER: I see. However, there are certain arrangements to be made, the marriage certificate, leg hobbles—but don't misunderstand me, the leg hobbles are not punitive, just a precaution against your running away.

MAN: Running away?

FATHER: Well, you have only to look at my daughter to understand the precaution.

MAN: Leg hobbles? How about the coitus? Or isn't that part of it?

FATHER: Aren't we getting a little ahead of ourselves?

MAN: Does she always do *it* on the floor?

FATHER: My daughter is merely being unconscious. You mustn't think she's trying to tempt you. Unfortunately, I was forced to take a little disciplinary action, and she blacked out.

[*The man sticks his tongue out and wags it, rolling his eyes and shaking his head.*]

FATHER: Why do you act like that?

MAN: Like what? [*He repeats what he did that made the father ask him why he acts the way he does.*]

FATHER [*with clinical interest*]: Like that.

MAN: Oh, if you don't like me I'll leave.

FATHER: No, no, now don't get like that; don't be so sensitive.

MAN: Maybe you want me to kiss your shoes? I will if you want.

FATHER: No, no! Don't start *that*.

MAN: No, no, really, I'm quite willing. I'll get right down on my hands and knees and crawl over to your feet. Really, it would be my pleasure.

FATHER: I said no; I do not require that.

40

MAN: Come on, I'm perfectly willing. [*Getting down on his hands and knees*] Look, see I'm on my hands and knees.

FATHER: Get the hell back on the couch! You act like a pervert.

MAN: Why? Just because I'm humble? Maybe you're working me up to something even more humiliating. I'm willing, you name it.

FATHER: I want you to marry my daughter; and I'll make a rich man of you.

MAN: Okay, okay, let's get it over with, drop your pants.

FATHER: What are you suggesting?!

MAN: I'm willing to do *it*, but I'm not going to talk about it.

FATHER: Would you like a punch in the face?!

MAN: Do I have to?

FATHER: Of course not! I asked you here for my daughter.

MAN: You mean *you* don't want me? [*He starts to cry.*]

FATHER: It isn't that, you're a lovely person, I'm sure; and if I were *that* way, why—

MAN [*sniffling*]: You're just saying that.

FATHER: No, I mean it. You could be quite attractive. Why, if you were only a woman, why, I—don't cry, after all, there are so many wonderful things in the world, ice cream sodas, rides on the carrousel—

MAN: No, no, you don't like me!

FATHER: I like you very much. But you see, I'm just not *that* way.

MAN: Oh yes you are! That's why it hurts.

FATHER: I am not! Even when I was a little boy my father used to say I was every inch a man. If anything, I have always

41

been overly masculine. Father even gave me a rifle to shoot when I was yet only a child.

MAN: But you look like my mother.

FATHER: Well, a man has a right to relax. Being a man is hard work. I've spent my life being overly masculine. Don't you think I have a right to be a woman at my age? I've earned it!

MAN: I want to be a woman, too.

FATHER: Well, you've got to earn it.

MAN: If I marry your daughter, then can I be a woman?

FATHER: Oh the devil take your conditions! Any other man would jump at the chance to be rich. Perhaps you like being poor?

MAN: I wouldn't be poor for all the money in the world. I'd do anything to be rich.

FATHER: You understand, then, that the marriage is binding, leg hobbles and all.

MAN: You can't expect me to crawl with leg hobbles; perhaps you plan to crawl to me?

FATHER: I do not crawl to any man! Perhaps my daughter will crawl to you.

MAN: Yes, we shall crawl together, like sisters, rivals for your affection, Daddy dear.

FATHER: I'm not taking you in as a daughter. I'm buying my own real daughter a husband!

MAN: Oh, will you buy me one, too?

FATHER: I don't owe you anything. Why should I buy you a husband?

MAN: If you expect me to be your daughter—

FATHER: But I don't expect you to be my daughter!

MAN: You don't like me. [*He begins to cry.*]

FATHER: Oh, don't start that again. Please. You're a very nice man.

MAN: No, you don't like me.

FATHER [*with a sour look*]: I think you're very nice.

MAN: Should I kiss your shoes? [*Getting on his hands and knees*]

FATHER: No, no, don't do that!

MAN: You're making a fool of me, you're one of those *cruel daddies*.

FATHER: Please, I don't mean to be cruel. When my daughter comes awake there'll be no end of things she'll let you do.

MAN: You brought me up here to ridicule me.

FATHER: No, please don't say that. [*He pets the man's head, who is still on his hands and knees.*]

[*The man kisses the father's hand with exaggerated affection.*]

FATHER [*withdrawing his hand with disgust*]: Don't do that!

MAN [*beginning to cry again*]: You don't like me.

FATHER: Well, the truth is, I don't. I just simply cannot like you.

MAN: You just brought me up here to humiliate me.

FATHER: I brought you up here? You came up here yourself, sir! I admit at my invitation, but for my daughter, only. You mustn't think—why, that's quite out of the question!

MAN [*still on his hands and knees*]: Now should I kiss your shoes?

FATHER: I'm getting rather sick of this. Are you going to marry my daughter or not?

MAN: That's how we arranged it, isn't it.

FATHER: Arranged what?

MAN: I could have been your secretary—

FATHER: I don't need a secretary!

MAN: And that's why I have to marry your daughter.

FATHER: That's not why! That has nothing to do with it!

MAN: Didn't you arrange it this way so I could be near you?

FATHER: What are you thinking?

MAN [*crying again*]: You don't like me. At the office, under those flattering fluorescent lights, you thought you liked me. But now, after seeing me in your home, you've decided against having me with you.

FATHER: Please don't cry. I think you're a lovely chap. [*Making a face as though having tasted something putrid*] But, it's my daughter who needs you.

MAN: You're not fooling me, that's your mother on the floor pretending to be unconscious. Anyway, your father would never give his wife's hand in marriage.

FATHER: My father has nothing to do with this. Besides, that's his granddaughter.

MAN: Wait a minute, this is a trap. You're a female cop disguised as this woman's grandfather.

FATHER: No, honestly, I'm the father. What is all this? Surely I don't look like a grandfather?

MAN: Sometimes it's a trick; you get invited someplace, and it turns out to be a trap; a policeman will pretend to be a man.

FATHER: Well, they are men. What are you talking about?

MAN: You're sure you're not a policewoman disguised as a businessman selling his daughter?

FATHER: Why are you so suspicious?

MAN: I've had trouble before.

FATHER: What trouble?

MAN: Never mind, that's why I carry a gun.

FATHER: A gun?! You're frightening me.

MAN: Scared, huh?

FATHER: I'm not afraid of you.

MAN: Please don't be afraid.

FATHER: I'm not afraid. Why should I be afraid?

MAN: No, really, I won't hurt you.

FATHER: I said I'm not afraid of you!

MAN: Admit it.

FATHER: Admit what?

MAN: You're afraid; it's natural.

DAUGHTER [*becoming conscious*]: Da da, goo goo . . .

FATHER: Do you want what she got?

MAN: What?

FATHER: A right to the stomach, and a left to the jaw!

MAN: You wouldn't hit me?

DAUGHTER: Da da [*Hiccup*] da da [*Hiccup*].

MAN: I'll kiss your shoes.

DAUGHTER [*hiccup, hiccup, hiccup*]: Goo.

MAN [*becoming aware of the baby sounds*]: What was that?

FATHER: Oh, I'm sorry. [*Gesturing toward his daughter*] This is my daughter. [*To his daughter*] And this is your future husband.

DAUGHTER [*reaching feebly out like an infant*]: Daddy, where are you?

FATHER [*smiling patronizingly; to the man*]: Help your darling up.

MAN [*looking at the daughter*]: Is it Mother?

FATHER: Mother of the species, heh heh.

DAUGHTER [*doing her "cute" baby act, hiccupping and burping, etc.*]: Da da, goo goo.

MAN: It's Mama! [*He runs to the daughter, and embraces and kisses her.*]

FATHER [*to the audience*]: It's disgusting.

DAUGHTER: Goo goo, da da.

MAN [*discovering that she is not his mother*]: You're not Mother! It's a trap!

DAUGHTER [*exaggerated sex stance*]: What's the difference, soldier boy?

MAN: No, no, you're not my mother!

DAUGHTER [*exaggerated sex stance*]: Come on, sailor boy.

FATHER [*to his daughter*]: Easy, easy; get the hook in his mouth.

DAUGHTER [*doing Mae West*]: Why don'tcha come up an' see me sometime?

FATHER: Easy, easy; let out some line.

MAN [*with a sudden change of pace, authoritative tone*]: Okay, this is an arrest. [*He pulls a badge out of his pocket.*]

FATHER: You're a cop!

MAN: That's right; attached to the morals squad. I'm going to have to run you in for suggestive obscenity.

FATHER: Your honor, I've done nothing. I plead innocent!

MAN: You've been suggesting all evening that I kiss your shoes.

FATHER: I asked you up here for my daughter.

MAN: Same thing: white slavery.

FATHER: But, but, but, but, but . . .

MAN: It's too late.

FATHER: No, wait, listen, I'll kiss your shoes if you'll only forget what you've seen.

MAN: Trying to bribe an officer: compounding the charges.

FATHER: All right, all right, I'll go down on my hands and knees.

MAN: You're only making it worse for yourself.

FATHER [*on his hands and knees*]: Look, I'll crawl over to your feet. Really, it would be my pleasure.

MAN: Can't you understand, the game is over? You're trapped.

FATHER: Come on, I'm perfectly willing. I'm on my hands and knees, I can crawl right over to your shoes.

DAUGHTER: Daddy!

FATHER: Not now, dear. [*To the man*] Working me up to something even more humiliating? I'm willing, you name it.

DAUGHTER: Daddy, he's mine!

FATHER: Not now, dear; can't you see I'm trying to avoid prison?

DAUGHTER: But he's mine!

FATHER: I'm fighting for my life, and all you can think is sex.

DAUGHTER: I want sex!

FATHER: I'll buy you all kinds of men. But now I'm fighting to clear my good name with the law. [*To the man*] Sir, please!

MAN: Look at my badge. [*Handing his badge to the father*] Would you have me disgrace it?

FATHER [*reading aloud from the badge*]: "Junior G-Man." [*Thoughtfully to himself*] An important man down on his hands and knees, begging to be humiliated. I can't believe that

47

a man of my importance is to be found on his hands and knees in front of his daughter's suitor, asking, begging.

MAN [*brightly*]: We all crawl one time or another, don't we, sir?

FATHER: You are quite right. I had forgotten how to crawl. Thank you for showing me again. I remember how I crawled up in the business world. I had quite a figure some years ago, and it didn't go unnoticed. I made important men sitting behind enormous desks crawl across their rugs to me. Of course I polished my shoes with hypnotic luster wax.

DAUGHTER: I want to crawl across the floor to him. [*Meaning her suitor; on her hands and knees*] Really, it would be my pleasure.

FATHER: People must crawl to me. Who of us has not got a crawling desire? Yet, who of us has the money to afford it? I can crawl, I proved that a few moments ago. But still, who knows which of us will not yet turn out to be a policeman?

DAUGHTER: But, Daddy, you said you were buying *me* a husband.

FATHER: Of course. But all this crawling business tends to ignite a certain crawling desire that begins at the feet. We are all crawlers at heart!

MAN: Don't let her crawl toward me!

FATHER: Things always look worse than they are. The thing is to face them. The imagination is far more fearful than reality.

MAN: No, no, I would crawl toward something. One has control that way. One can always stop and go the other way.

FATHER: Yes, yes, we like to crawl toward things. That's how we keep things from crawling toward us. You are so right!

DAUGHTER [*mistaking her father for her suitor*]: May I crawl to you?

FATHER: Oh no, dear child, for as attractive as—

48

DAUGHTER: Really, it would be my pleasure.

FATHER: Oh no, dear child, for as attractive as—

DAUGHTER: I'm humble, but maybe you're working me up to something even more humiliating?

FATHER: Oh no, dear child, for as attractive as—

DAUGHTER: Okay, okay, I'm willing, let's get it over with, drop your pants.

FATHER: Oh no, dear child, for as attractive as your offer may seem, still, the biology of our relationship, and the differences in our ages, not to mention the illegality, or the fact that you are most unattractive, being in your forties and quite over-weight, and the late hour, and a number of other things that work against such a consummation. Besides which, I'M YOUR FATHER!

DAUGHTER [*surprised recognition*]: *Father?!* But, you said you were going to marry me.

FATHER [*pointing to the man*]: He's going to marry you.

DAUGHTER: Then why are you trying to humiliate me, making me crawl to *you*?

FATHER: No such a thing! I was trying to keep you off.

DAUGHTER: Why do you want to hurt me, just when I'm trying to be attractive. You don't know how lonely I've been. Men like women to crawl to them.

FATHER: But I'm a married man. Don't you remember, I married your mother some years ago.

DAUGHTER: Da da [*Hiccup*] goo goo, da da.

FATHER: No, no, not that way.

DAUGHTER: Then what way? You don't want me to crawl, and you don't want me to be cute.

MAN: Is it my turn?

FATHER: For what?

MAN: To crawl.

FATHER: To whom?

MAN: One just crawls. There's no other way.

FATHER: Why does everyone have to crawl? There are so many other ways: ice cream sodas, rides on the carrousel.

DAUGHTER: But doesn't it make the woman's arse so much more attractive if it grinds along humiliated in the dust of human approval? Besides, it's nice to be close to the ground in case there's some change lying around.

FATHER: But you're a rich woman, you don't need change.

DAUGHTER: Everyone needs some change. Do you think I want to go on like this the rest of my life?

MAN: And what of me? I'm not a rich woman.

FATHER: You're not a woman.

MAN: That doesn't mean I couldn't do with some change.

FATHER: Yes, that makes sense, we could all do with a change.

[*They all get down on their hands and knees and crawl off the stage.*]

CURTAIN

The Children

The Children

This one-act entertainment takes place in an old-fashioned living room of stuffed furniture and bric-a-brac, all somewhat faded. The characters are members of an aging family: A mother and father in their eighties, and their two children, a son and daughter, both well into their sixties.

[As we discover them the father is reading a newspaper, his son sits, resting his chin and hands on the head of a cane, absorbed in his own thoughts; his sister also seems isolated in her thoughts as she works on an embroidery. The mother studies her children, one and then the other, smiling warmly with pride and satisfaction.]

MOTHER [*brightly*]: Just look at our fine children! Both so accomplished at sitting pleasantly in a room. And just look how Daughter's grey hair complements the wallpaper. How tastefully her hair blends with the evening newspaper. Something so dry and papery about her hair—just lovely! And our son; how I worried when his hair started falling out. I thought he'd look like an old meany. But look how dignified. It breaks my heart to see such a handsome boy. I suppose I'll just have to hide him from the girls.

FATHER: Oh yes, Mother, I think we did a pretty good job with the children, they've really turned out fine. They'll thank us one day, I'm sure. [*To his daughter*] Sweetheart, after all these years of reflection, aren't you glad that we broke up that childish infatuation you had? What was it, thirty years ago? Why, just think, you might have married that young fool.

53

DAUGHTER [*without expression*]: Yes, Father, I have always been grateful to you.

FATHER [*to his son*]: And do you remember how I saved you from that awful girl you were getting too serious with? Your papa has always been in there seeing that you kids got only the best.

SON [*bored resigned voice*]: Yes, Father, youthful folly.

MOTHER: Certainly, my dears, you've plenty of time; let the others rush into marriage.

DAUGHTER: I have my embroidery.

FATHER: And I think your *home sweet home* is really beautiful.

MOTHER: Her *home is where the heart is* is equally as beautiful, if not more so.

FATHER [*to his son*]: And you, how do you occupy your days?

SON: Sometimes I walk in the park. Sometimes I just lean on my cane and stand in the sun; a before-dinner nap . . . I manage to fill my days.

MOTHER [*brightly*]: Just look at daughter's lovely grey hair! It just seems part of the wallpaper. Doesn't it do something for this room? I always think of Mother when I look at Daughter; Mother was a beautiful old lady. [*Meaning her daughter*] Look how her grey dress, her grey hair, yes, even her face, just seem to be part of the wallpaper.

FATHER [*to his daughter*]: Yes, I certainly must compliment you on the way you just seem part of the furnishings. Some people are just too vivid, they fairly sparkle. One finds one's attention drawn to them; terribly annoying when one is trying to read the newspaper. You are certainly a comfort, sometimes I'm not even aware you're in the room.

SON: Yes, Sister, you're as shabby as everything else in this room. You look like Mother's mother, and I suppose I look like her father. [*To his parents*] Your compliments are really sickening. What consolation is it to hear over and over again how shabby one is. I've had none of the joys that are the true consolation of old age. I don't mean to complain, only, it's difficult enough to bear without false praise, compliments that only point up what they thinly disguise. Look at my sister, she's on her sixty-third *home is where the heart is.*

MOTHER: No, no, dear, you're wrong.

SON: *Of course I'm wrong.*

MOTHER: No, I mean you're wrong because you're young; young people are always too impatient.

SON: I'm not a young person. I'm proportionately closer to your's and father's age that I am to being young. That's all behind me! Can't you see that by constantly referring to me as a young person you force me to remember how old I am? Why, I don't even have the dreams of a young man.

FATHER: Balderdash! Why, when I was your age—

SON: Your children were already entering middle age.

FATHER: Well—yes, but only because I dashed into marriage while I was still young and foolish. Sure, it turned out all right. But, supposing it hadn't?

SON: It still would've been right. It's what men and women are supposed to do. We're not born only to get old with nothing between birth and death.

FATHER: I think that's pretty insulting: How dare you play so loosely with your mother's and my happiness? Implying that the beautiful life your mother and I have enjoyed has no special value beyond the simple animal vulgarities.

SON: No, no, I mean—of course, it is of greatest value. But I mean that a bad marriage is better than no marriage, the loneliness—I have never been with a woman. I have nothing to remember of women except my mother's kisses.

FATHER [*angry*]: That's barroom talk! That's dirty and unworthy of our home!

DAUGHTER: Please, please, I stuck my finger with the needle; my embroidery is spoilt with blood.

SON: You'll do another, and another, and another . . .

MOTHER [*to her son*]: How can you say that?—Each one is different and more beautiful than the last . . . And her beautiful grey hair . . . Our lovely home . . . Why do you want to shout?! Are we so old that we can't hear you perfectly well when you speak in the cultured way you were brought up to speak?

DAUGHTER [*sadly*]: No, no, it's ruined with blood; I'll have to start again.

FATHER: Oh dear, too bad . . . [*To his son*] Please, let's not argue, we're ruining your sister's work. [*To his daughter*] And do you know what I think, I think one day your embroideries will be considered real works of art—I really think so . . . [*She begins to sob.*] . . . Now, now, don't cry, many artists have had one of their works spoilt, but they did others . . . You know, I think your embroidery is even better than Mother's . . .

MOTHER: Well, what do you want? I've never had time to sit down long enough; raising the children, and times weren't always that good. Not that it wasn't fun, it was: Saving to buy a bedspread, or to get you that new suit. Remember how we saved, cheating on the meatloaf, a little more bread, a little less meat. It tasted just as good. Those were good old days. But learning to embroider as beautifully as Daughter, I guess not. Perhaps in the next life.

FATHER [*to his sobbing daughter*]: Don't cry, dear, Mother doesn't mean those were such hard times that we didn't have fun. Really, they weren't that bad. We had you kids, and they were really some of the best days of our lives. I remember how your mother and I would sit in the evening, after you children were in bed, and sometimes we'd talk until morning. I didn't seem to get as tired then. We'd have breakfast together, before you children were up, and I'd go to the office and do a whole day's work without a yawn. When you're young you don't know what *tired* is. These days I welcome the bed.

MOTHER [*to her son*]: You know who you look like? What's his name? . . . Uh . . .

SON: Oh don't start that now; you always start that!

MOTHER: No, no, not him—George Washington! You look just like George Washington. Yes you do! Very distinguished. [*To her husband*] Doesn't he look like George Washington?

FATHER: . . . Something similar. The bald head and the grey hair. Yes, I see what you mean.

SON: Oh, what is this? So I look like a bald-headed man. I am bald!

FATHER: Oh, don't be such a sourpuss.

MOTHER [*to her son*]: You do seem awfully irritable, dear. Perhaps you need a physic. Maybe you have a temperature. Let me feel your head. [*She tries to touch his forehead.*]

SON [*Shrugging away*]: Mother, please, I don't look like George Washington and I don't have a fever!

FATHER: Really, Son, you have been acting strange lately . . . Is it a girl?

SON: At my age?

FATHER: Listen to the boy, *at his age!* You've got all the symptoms of a young buck kicking up his heels. Look, he's blushing!

SON: I haven't blushed for forty years.

FATHER: Now listen, my boy, we're with you, we understand. You go kick up your heels a little, it's about time. But just see that you use a little judgment. But I don't have to tell you this, you're a decent kid.

SON: Will you stop it! You go on and on!

FATHER: What do you mean I go on and on? I'm just trying to understand you, and you tell me to butt out of your business. I'm not trying to tell you what to do. I just hope there'll never come a time when you feel you can't talk to us. A good-looking guy like you is bound to have a girl or two. I'm not censuring you. Remember, I was once young, too.

SON: There you go, calling me a young fellow who can't keep the girls off, as if I were twenty. I'm sixty-seven. I'm glad to make it to the park and back. Kick up my heels?—I have trouble just balancing on them. You go on and on and on.

FATHER: Well, I guess I know when to butt out.

SON: There's nothing to butt out of.

FATHER: Okay, okay, I can take a hint.

MOTHER: Your father doesn't mean to butt into your affairs, he's just interested in you. It wouldn't hurt you to ask for a little fatherly advice once in awhile. After all, you've had very little experience with the world. One can get his heart broken pretty easily. I know you're far too much of a gentleman to ever take advantage of a girl. But these days there are many unscrupulous girls.

FATHER: That's just what I meant, Mother. It's not just an old man's idle curiosity when he inquires about his son. [*To his son*] Now take your sister, for instance, we all know she has a beau. She makes no secret of it. But you don't see her getting all cranky. And we're willing to wait for her to decide the right time for us to meet her young man.

SON: Sister's an old spinster. No man has looked at her for thirty years; she never leaves the house. What *are* you talking about?

FATHER: Do you mean a beautiful girl like your sister has no suitors? Really, you are too selfish with your opinion. You're so busy looking after your own love-life you haven't had time to notice your sister. Why, just the other day I saw a blond young man passing the house. I saw the way he looked at the house, it was unmistakable.

SON: A blond young man? Look at her, she's probably old enough to be his grandmother.

MOTHER: How can you say such a thing? Does your sister tease you about being overweight? About being so clumsy you can barely get upstairs? Why, your father can negotiate the stairs better than you.

FATHER [*to his son*]: I think your remarks are pretty rotten, I really do. You know how sensitive a woman is about her age. Not that your sister needs to be; why, she's just reaching her womanly prime.

MOTHER: I think somebody ought to go to his room, and stay there until he has something pleasant to say.

[*The son leaves, and is heard climbing the stairs off stage.*]

MOTHER [*to her daughter*]: Dear, sit with us.

FATHER: Yes, sit with us, sweetheart.

[*The daughter sits between them on the couch.*]

MOTHER: I love the way you're wearing your hair.

[*The daughter's grey hair is worn with the severity of the typical spinster. She touches her hair and shyly looks away.*]

FATHER: Yes, dear, you look very sweet. You make your father very proud.

MOTHER: And that dress, it looks just lovely. [*The dress is grey and out of fashion.*] I don't think I've seen it before.

DAUGHTER: I have two others like it.

MOTHER: Really? Then the lace collar is new.

DAUGHTER: No, it came with the dress.

MOTHER: Well, then it's your hair. That makes all the difference!

DAUGHTER: Father . . . I . . .

FATHER: I know, you want me to meet your young man.

DAUGHTER: I . . .

59

FATHER: It's perfectly natural. In the spring the boy bird and the girl bird build a nest. Bring him around anytime, I'd be more than glad to discuss his financial position, his family, and all his other credentials. Don't worry, dear, I'm not an old-fashioned father type, I know what it is to be young and in love.

DAUGHTER: But . . .

FATHER: —He hasn't made his pot of gold yet. Okay, there's time. Listen, dear, a poor boy can go just as far as a rich boy. The big thing is ambition. Without that I don't care how much money you have. What good is it? No sirree! The man on his way is the man I take my hat off to. No, no, you're right to choose a poor boy with plenty of drive. Well, I never did worry about you when it came to marriage. A girl with your looks doesn't have to wait long, and plenty to choose from, too. A lot of girls have to settle with what they can have; and damned lucky to get that. So, if by some odd luck I don't think he's right for you, you mustn't worry, there're plenty of fish in the ocean.

MOTHER: Oh, men, they go on about things that only women understand. [*To her husband*] I think you had better let me talk to our young lady. Why don't you see what that naughty boy is doing. Maybe a father and son talk would do him some good.

FATHER [*getting up*]: Yes, dear.

[*He squeezes his daughter's hand, and kisses her on her head, and leaves. He is heard off stage climbing the stairs with more energy than his son.*]

MOTHER: You know, dear, you ought really to start thinking seriously about marriage. Of course you're not *that* old, but a girl should look ahead a little. Life is not all roses and moonbeams.

DAUGHTER: But, Mother . . . [*Starting to cry*]

MOTHER: I know growing up is difficult. But, to be frank, you can no longer afford to indulge idle flirtations. Time is life. Life must be lived in the time alotted to it. There's the raising of children; living to see one's grandchildren. You play too long. The roses fade. What one took in youth as value fades with youth. And there is nothing wrong with comfort. As you get older you will see that comfort is the true value. For as you get older it becomes harder and harder to be comfortable. The flesh is full of hurts that age uncovers.

DAUGHTER: Mother . . . [*Shaking her head and crying*] . . . Mother . . .

MOTHER: Lately, dear, you have developed the rather unattractive habit of crying. Men run away from women who cry. It is useful sometimes in winning a point. But the instrument is dulled by constant use. As to the original point of our discussion, your father will listen to me as to the proper husband for you. As to the young man . . .

DAUGHTER: There *is* no young man.

MOTHER: Oh come, dear, I'm your mother. I hope there won't be any secrets between us.

DAUGHTER: There is no one.

MOTHER: No one at *all*?

DAUGHTER: Not for years and years and years . . .

MOTHER: What are you saying?

[*The daughter begins to weep with heavy sobbing.*]

MOTHER: Oh, stop that unattractive crying! Nothing makes a woman seem so disgusting as constant sniffling.

DAUGHTER: Please, I can't talk anymore, please!

MOTHER: Can't talk?! Time is running out, my dear. Life is choice. One must choose. One must act!

DAUGHTER: Mother . . .

MOTHER [*as if in a trance*]: One does not ask to be born. No, my dear, one is awakened, as it were, from the vast dreamless sleep of the universe, and particularized as hope and fear. Childhood seems endless. But time is swift. The little girl is the woman. Modesty, sensitivity, are put by for function. One surveys life, its repetitions, its injustices. One decides in favor of *having*. Yes, my dear, many starve that the few might privilege. It is the law, written in the stars, that energy, and only energy shall be rewarded; that the weak shall feed the strong. One decides to be strong. One asks now to be born. One chooses to be in life, and to gather all the good things that life can offer. The woman is born with a sensitivity that seeks the quiet, the gentle; and this is how she loses against the aggressiveness that is the man. The secret of successful womanhood is that the woman becomes a *man*. Because men are born men they neglect this study. And this is our advantage. Your father, unbeknownst to him, takes a *man* to bed with him. You are of an age that this secret should be yours. Do not blush, my awkward girl. This, that is between the man and the woman, is the woman's first power, and the loss of the man's. They climb upon the woman as joyful conquerors. But the woman is like a vast country, and can absorb this insult upon her modesty. She can absorb the very conqueror. She outlasts him. Womanizes him. The woman in her age grows strong, the man weak. And time is always hers. Women love their sons, seeing them before they are proud. In their weakness we pity them, and this is love. If women despise their daughters it is because, to be strong, they have had to despise themselves. But it comes to be the time when the *king* must pass the secret of the power to his *son:* The chain of the sisterhood continues. Daughters and mothers are equals, and therefore rivals. The universe entrusts to our keeping the city of man . . . You are blessed with beauty and a flair for clothes. These are tools, my dear, these are teeth and claws.

DAUGHTER [*weeping*]: No, Mother, no!

MOTHER: No *what?*

DAUGHTER: The paradox is impossible with me, I'm not even a woman.

MOTHER: You were born a woman. You have no choice, you are the heir apparent!

62

DAUGHTER: I was born with something to fill. I have neglected to become anything. I am a feminine thing without a person.

MOTHER: You are a person! A female person! My daughter!

DAUGHTER [*stops crying, very soberly*]: No. I am one of a household of old people. I am a furniture . . . At first I was only afraid. I was young then. I remember standing naked before a mirror looking at the woman I had become, confused and panicked. The window behind me showed a bough of blossoms. I stood a long time looking at my breasts and my thighs, like a little girl looking on a naked woman; mentally pasting a male image upon the image in the mirror. Touching myself in such a way to know *how* it must be. And I knew, even in the excitement of my want, that I would never say *yes*. I hoped time would change this. I dreamed of being forced. And I knew I would never say *yes*. You and Father helped me by keeping the young men away. I was relieved many times from not having to say *no*. You and Father said it for me. And I grew to hate you both. With time the excitment of my want grew less. And with that the greater panic, that I was going to die without having lived. I wore clothes too old for me, and acted *the old woman* long before I was an old woman; thus have I become an old woman without ever having been a young woman. I put my life to sleep long ago. You and Father continued to refer to me as a child. And there was comfort in this. It meant you could not see me dying, that you had never seen me. And I did not want to be seen, or judged, or pitied . . . The problem is that life is too long, the decision is weakened by time. Just when it is too late one wishes it weren't.

MOTHER [*slapping her daughter*]: I'll make you live!

DAUGHTER: No, don't make me hurt anyone. [*Weeping*] I want to be loved . . . I want to die!

MOTHER: You bitch! You filthy harlot bitch! You'd cocktease the universe!

FATHER [*suddenly returning*]: Hey, hey, what's going on with my girls?

63

MOTHER: This dirty bitch is a cocktease!

FATHER: A *what*-tease? What are you saying?!

MOTHER: You know what I'm saying, you pig!

FATHER: *Pig?* Have you had a stroke?

MOTHER: A stroke, is it?!—You pervert!

FATHER: My God, Mother, what's come over you?

MOTHER: Oh isn't her hair beautiful—*Queen* of the May! Bitch, bitch, bitch, with her foul puss!

FATHER: Mother, I demand that you stop!

MOTHER: *You demand*, you, you dirty old woman?!

[*While the daughter wails and beats on the wall, her brother is heard coming downstairs.*]

SON [*entering*]: What happened?

FATHER [*weeping*]: I don't know.

MOTHER: The other pervert!

SON: Mother!

MOTHER: Why don't you go to the park and sit with the other masturbators?

SON [*he starts to struggle with his mother, rolling on the floor with her.*] You bitch! You dirty rotten bitch!

FATHER [*banging his fist in time with his words*]: Get off your mother. In spite of everything you cannot fight your mother, because nothing will be left . . . Everything washing out to sea . . . Get off your mother because the world is ending.

DAUGHTER [*approaching her father with a knife*]: I'm going to cut your Adam's apple out because it's a testicle.

FATHER: What?! What?! Give me that knife! [*He rolls on the floor with her, fighting for the knife.*] Think I don't know you have men in your room, you slut!

64

[*The mother and daughter are getting the best of the father and son.*]

FATHER: I give up! I give up!

[*Both men are on their feet, backing up as the women advance.*]

FATHER: Have pity, after all, we're of a family. Doesn't the father image have some meaning? For the sake of family symmetry let's not destroy the paterfamilias!

MOTHER: I'm the father image, the paterfamilias!

FATHER: Yes, dear.

MOTHER [*nudging her daughter*]: And this here's my son.

DAUGHTER: That's right, you sluts.

[*The father and son giggle like maidens.*]

MOTHER: You two females are gonna wear skirts.

FATHER: If modesty demands it.

MOTHER: *I* demand it!

SON: We're so old what does it matter, anyway?

MOTHER: It's a new beginning.

FATHER: A new birth.

SON: I'm scared.

FATHER: These strong *men* will protect us.

[*The father and son giggle like maidens.*]

MOTHER: Enough of that, you big-hipped cows. [*To her daughter, who has begun to embroider again*] Put that down! Am I the only man here?! [*Again to her daughter*] Come on, let's go out and get a piece of ass.

[*The mother and daughter leave.*]

[*The father picks up his newspaper and begins to read. His son rests his hands and chin on the head of his cane.*]

FATHER [*after a short pause*]: The house seems so empty without them.

[*His son nods thoughtfully.*]

FATHER: Did I ever talk to you about, about, love—sexual love?

[*His son sighs a distracted sigh.*]

FATHER: Now that your sister is married . . . Didn't she marry that blond boy we used to see passing the house?

SON: Isn't she down town shopping for some more thread with mother?

FATHER: That's right. But doesn't the house seem empty without them?

[*The son yawns.*]

FATHER: Sex—your mother's a *man*.

SON: At her age does it matter?

FATHER: I suppose in the end all definitions merge. They seem so important in the beginning.

[*The son sighs.*]

FATHER: You seem to do a lot of sighing.

SON: It's a way of filling conversational space.

FATHER: That's an old man's trick.

[*The son sighs again.*]

FATHER: There, you've done it again. Your mother's a man . . . That makes me a woman.

SON: Oh, Father, I don't care.

FATHER: But it's important.

SON: Why?

FATHER: Because we cannot escape the universe. And it's not right just to simply sigh. The universe is parts that fit together, as in and out, lost and found, male and female. We cannot escape it!

SON: But do we have to think about it? Can't the universe do it without us?

FATHER: But, don't you see that—

[*The mother and daughter suddenly return.*]

DAUGHTER [*to her mother*]: Rhetorical nonsense! You're no more a *man* than Father.

MOTHER: Shut up, you bitch!

DAUGHTER: If the paradox of the woman becoming the man had any truth, that would leave you out. You've never even been a woman!

MOTHER: That's not true, these breasts have meant something in the world. [*She makes her breasts prominent.*]

DAUGHTER: They're meaningless to me, *Mother dear.*

MOTHER: You think you look any better, *dearie*?

DAUGHTER: We look of an age, old unmarried sisters.

MOTHER: But I have a husband. And I've used my puss for more than something to hide in my bloomers.

FATHER: [*to his daughter as though to a child*]: Mother's right.

[*All nod thoughtfully, as if in agreement. Then each of them breaks out in quiet, private weeping. They find their original places: The daughter embroidering, the father reading his newspaper, and his son sitting again, leaning his hands and chin on his cane; the mother once more studying her children with warm smiling pride.*]

MOTHER [*brightly*]: Just look at our fine children! Both so accomplished at sitting pleasantly in a room. And just look how daughter's grey hair complements the wallpaper. How tastefully her hair blends with the evening newspaper. Something so dry and papery about her hair—just lovely! And our son; how I worried when his hair started falling out. I thought he'd look like an old meany. But look how dignified. It breaks my heart to see such a handsome boy. I suppose I shall just have to hide him from the girls.

FATHER: Oh yes, Mother, I think we did a pretty good job with the children, they've really turned out fine. They'll thank us one day, I'm sure. [*To his daughter*] Sweetheart, after all these years of reflection, aren't you glad that we broke up that childish infatuation you had? What was it, thirty years ago? Why, just think, you might have married that young fool . . .

CURTAIN

Ketchup

Ketchup

This is a five-part amusement about a family [a set of parents, both middle-aged, and their two sons, Percival and Oscar, men in their late thirties] who are forced to a tragic awareness by one misstep taken by the father, while wearing a pair of English Oxfords. Out of a life of previous complacence and duteous repetition, this one misstep puts at risk his wife's home-bottled ketchup, and the careers of his sons, not to mention their well-to-do middle class home, where the melancholy events pictured in this amusement unfold.

PART ONE

FATHER [*frightened and out of breath, he has just come into the house; even so, he delivers himself with a kind of rhetorical matter-of-factness*]: I'm afraid a rather dangerous situation has developed between ourselves and our neighbors. As I was moving from one point to another, in my usual attempt to process myself through the efficiency that the shortest distance between two points is a straight line, when returning from the office to our lovely home. But luck ran out. What served as the habit of the years, the to and fro of my coming and going, save Sundays and other holidays, not to mention sick days, or to mention sick days, as evidence of a failing health, has all come to an abrupt and unseemly end.

MOTHER: Oh, Father, Father, what cruel thing have you brought upon us?

FATHER: I stepped on the neighbor's child. It lay in my path. I calculated: Will I be able to avoid it? No, it seemed that I would not. Perhaps I shall be able to step over it? Confusion and doubt grew strong in me. As a high jumper paces his stride to the bar—but no, as I drew upon the child I saw it was too late. One of my beautiful new English Oxfords went squarely on the child. I feared that I might slip.

MOTHER: It can be dangerous.

FATHER: The neighbors started to run after me. Now I increased my gait. I was running.

MOTHER: Oh, Father, at your age that's a dangerous thing.

FATHER: However, the male neighbor seemed more threat than the exertion to remove myself from the immediate range of his rage.

MOTHER: Good thinking, Father.

FATHER: Thank you, my dear. We shall, of course, have to close the shutters on the windows.

MOTHER: But my beautiful curtains . . . When people pass the house they say, "The woman has beautiful curtains, she must be a beautiful woman."

FATHER: Hard times. And we shall have to build a dummy and fill it with ketchup. We'll put it out in the yard some night for the male neighbor to vent his anger on; something that will seem to bleed.

MOTHER: Not all my home-bottled ketchup? No, that's too cruel! How will I eat beans and steak? What will spinach taste like without ketchup?

FATHER: Hard times. Even I am contributing my best suit to the dummy; the one I had planned to be buried in . . . There is a certain justice in this; I haven't time to work out the quid pro quos of it.

MOTHER: But why should the dummy demand all our things?

FATHER: It's a sacrifice, it gives it's life for mine. Dare we do less for one who is to be the victim of the male neighbor?

MOTHER: Perhaps if you apologized on the telephone?

FATHER: He might hang up on me.

MOTHER: Rudeness is unforgivable.

FATHER: Hard times, people become rude.

MOTHER: And our children, how shall they grow up to be useful citizens?

FATHER: They'll have to give it up.

MOTHER: Give up what?

FATHER: Growing up, or becoming useful citizens, they can't do both. Hard times teach us that what we took for granted never took us so.

MOTHER: And they so wanted to be useful citizens.

FATHER: Well, Mother, in a country as rich as this they can still get along without being useful.

MOTHER: Perhaps you could go to the male neighbor and offer yourself in place of his child.

FATHER: No, Mother, it's not dignified. Even in hard times one must try to maintain some dignity.

MOTHER: Of course, Father, and I think it was a girl-child, anyway. I think you would be the wrong sex.

FATHER: Why are you bringing up sex at a time like this?

MOTHER: I only meant—

FATHER: That's the trouble with you, you speak before you think.

MOTHER: But, Father, I only meant—

FATHER: That's exactly the trouble with you! Now that we've come upon hard times, now, more than ever, we need to stick together. And what do you do?

MOTHER: Oh, Father, what shall we do?

FATHER: As our energies permit, we must bring all our resources to play. The house must be made into a fort. We shall say our prayers before bed, regularly. Not that I place much benefit to this procedure, but there's no use in missing out on a protective measure by being too smart. It's dangerous to be too smart.

MOTHER: Then it's smart not to be too smart?

FATHER: Now don't get smart with me!

MOTHER: I only meant—

FATHER: That's the trouble with you, you talk before you think. Before you apply any moral censorship your mouth is open, and the foulest implications are falling out of it.

MOTHER: But, Father—

FATHER: But Father *nothing!* Enough of these excuses and dodges. If you cannot see the extreme danger to our house because of the male neighbor, not to mention his wife, the female neighbor—why, how do I know they haven't got relatives scattered around the neighborhood, positioned that they could not attack the house from all directions? My God! And all you want to talk about is sex! What on earth could sex mean to me at a time like this; or, incidentally, at my age? My God, you haven't talked about sex for twenty years. Why now? Just when I'm trying to save the house!

MOTHER: Why are you yelling at me? Did I step on the neighbor's child? Did I set the male neighbor against you? You did these things, and you yell at me, expecting my loyalty.

FATHER: Mother, forgive me, you can see I'm terribly nervous.

MOTHER: Of course, dear . . . And, after all, being a useful citizen isn't everything; surely, being an unuseful citizen must have some use?

FATHER: How can being unuseful be useful? Do you see how you attack, how you whittle down my mental energies?!

MOTHER: I only meant—

FATHER: You see, you see, again you only *meant?* Why do you make me fight you? You know how at odds with the world I am. Why are you so disloyal?

MOTHER: I was only trying to rationalize a situation being forced on our children. After all, they've spent their whole lives looking forward to being useful citizens.

FATHER: Hard times, Mother, hard times . . .

MOTHER: And whose fault?

FATHER: See? You're accusing me!

MOTHER: Well, you see, the children did want to be useful citizens, which would have made me the mother of useful citizens: A very useful mother. But, as it is now, all we can hope for is the preservation of our lives. And, since we are getting old and shall lose them anyway, what's the use?

FATHER: Oh, so you *are* blaming me.

MOTHER: What good is blame, what's done is done.

FATHER: You blame to find the wound, to say, "Here, this is the hurtful spot, this is the injury." The mind rests easier when it finds the object of its disquiet.

MOTHER: Hush, Father, you're about to say something ugly.

FATHER: Does it occur to you that the male neighbor is stronger than I am, that he will run right over me and rape you?

MOTHER: Which is his right.

FATHER: What right has he to rape you?!

MOTHER: The right of the victor.

FATHER: Are you *turning?*

MOTHER: But where's the necessity to use all my home-bottled ketchup?

FATHER: Is there any question about its use if it decoys away the blow meant for me?

MOTHER: But you know how I hate spinach without ketchup.

FATHER: Do you understand that I want to use the ketchup instead of my own blood?

MOTHER: But Father, you have your own blood, why do you want to involve the ketchup?

FATHER: Because ketchup is less dear than blood.

MOTHER: I worked so hard to bottle that ketchup.

FATHER: Would you rather my blood to the ketchup?

MOTHER: Now that's silly; of course not. It's just that I don't want you to ruin my ketchup just for spite.

FATHER: Shut up, you do not understand me!

MOTHER: Perhaps if you went to the male neighbor and apologized—

FATHER: Apologize?! Are you crazy? Something wrong with your head? I'd have about as much dignity left as an old worn-out English Oxford. In hard times one has only his dignity.

[*There is the sound of a shell whistling through the air, which ends with a rock coming through the window; in the background distant small arms' fire, with perhaps a bugle playing the call that signals the charge.*]

FATHER [*gravely*]: And so it begins . . . At this time I wish to make a statement—

MOTHER: Say something! Just look at the window!

FATHER [*gravely*]: A state of war exists between ourselves and those who inhabit the adjoining property. And, as your leader, I call upon the members of this household to have courage, and to remember *that blood is thicker than ketchup!*

MOTHER: No it's not.

FATHER: Never mind, every war has to have a slogan.

MOTHER: Look, Father, there's a note tied to the rock.

FATHER [*picking up the rock*]: Maybe they wish to surrender.

MOTHER: What does it say?

FATHER [*he reads the note*]: . . . They want our *unconditional* surrender.

MOTHER: What does that mean?

FATHER: Oh shut up!

[*The house is wrecked, and their clothes are torn and soiled. In the background, at low level, are the sounds of war, with flashing lights.*]

FATHER [*impatiently*]: Where's the dummy?

MOTHER [offstage]: I'm bringing it. [*She drags the dummy onto the stage.*]

FATHER [*seeing the dummy*]: That's not me!

MOTHER: No, no, nor was it meant to be, no more than you were meant to be in the beginning.

FATHER: No, no, it flatters nothing; nor does it extend, by any means, native luck—the indigenous resplendency, that grace more than nature first endows.

MOTHER: It's stuffed with brassières, women's drawers and enema bags of ketchup, rubber prophylactics, children's balloons, all stuffed with ketchup: Token gut of man!

FATHER: That's not me!

MOTHER: Nor was it meant more than any of us in the endless repetition.

FATHER: Without flattery!

MOTHER: Without insult.

FATHER: There's no middle ground: Without flattery, it insults.

MOTHER: It is a victim.

FATHER: Oh, I see, not that I do the act, but that I deliver him who is done the act, so am I guilty . . .

MOTHER: Guilty? [*Distractedly*] It is to be seen as the tumblers in a lock, each falling through a predicted portion, each event upon a single axle falls predicted, and the lock falls free and the future swings out, and you see as through an open door.

FATHER: No, no, I wish only to study an interior of walls. No, no, I have no wish for doors. If one is guilty he wishes only to

77

look at wallpaper; in wallpaper are things right: There the milk-maid and all her sisters bear yokes of milk through the facsimile summer . . . One would give long periods of life to wondering about the happenings behind the doorframe where the wall-paper disappears: There, naked milkmaids have put down their yokes and roll about in the grass of the facsimile summer, re-vealing those parts which differ markedly from equally luscious boys . . . And to spend days thusly, in so refusing else than this . . .

MOTHER: But doesn't the male neighbor grow great with wrath, like a long endured female anger, practicing your death a thousand times?

FATHER: Parturition! Of course he does. Did he not always? Doesn't any neighbor practice the death of his neighbor? Does not any neighbor, given right by an act of his neighbor, rejoice in the act that vents his desire?

MOTHER: Oh, Father, you make the world so terrible.

FATHER: Why do you turn against me in the moment of crisis, when your love is of greatest premium? When, without it I have only myself, whom I cannot find. Though I search myself I cannot find myself. In all memory I see only events peopled by others, and I cannot find myself. Mother, where am I?

MOTHER [*pointing to the wallpaper, consolingly*]: Look, dear, the milkmaids: One learns a certain bravery there; they look not to the future, nor do they look out of the past, but, in the moment that is the lifetime of a family; they carry milk up the hills to those little houses. One wonders if in those little houses there are not walls covered with milkmaids carrying milk to houses with even smaller milkmaids on their walls, carrying milk to yet even smaller—

FATHER: Stop it! Stop it! You're making me dainty with intro-spection while the male neighbor is moving upon the house. He has a knife to see if I bleed blood. Or, shall I ooze with ketchup?

MOTHER: Well, put the dummy outside!

FATHER: Is it night yet?

MOTHER: Do you have eyes?

FATHER: Why are you talking *fresh?*

MOTHER: I'm sorry. I try, but every so often I despise you.

FATHER: Just when I need your love.

MOTHER: I try, but every so often . . .

FATHER: Again I stand alone; whoever I am, I stand alone.

MOTHER: Oh, Father, am I not here standing next to you?

FATHER: Not really, even I have run away from myself. I should put myself out in the yard instead of the dummy.

MOTHER: It's getting dark.

FATHER [*he takes the dummy under its arms and drags it to the door*]: I suppose it's time to put the dummy out?

MOTHER: Poor thing.

FATHER: Would you rather I put myself out?

MOTHER: Make it comfortable.

FATHER: It's not alive!

MOTHER: No, I suppose not.

FATHER: You suppose?!

MOTHER: Don't press me, Father!

FATHER: Press you?

MOTHER: Go along, don't make it any harder than it is.

FATHER: What's hard about putting a dummy out to save your husband's life?

MOTHER: Enough! Just put it out!

[*He drags the dummy out of the door.*]

PART THREE

[*Several weeks have passed, and the war seems to be over. They are wearing fresh clothes, and the house has been restored.*]

MOTHER: Is the peace difficult?

FATHER: Not when one remembers the difficulty of war.

MOTHER: But one forgets, getting further and further away from the hardship.

FATHER: It's unpatriotic not to remember the dead, and the sacrifices of the living.

MOTHER: Is the peace difficult?

FATHER: I just said it shouldn't be.

MOTHER: But if the glands be still at the ready?

FATHER: Be quiet!

MOTHER: But the glands.

FATHER: Let them sweat!

MOTHER: But if the heart is not ready to conclude its expectations?

FATHER: Expectations?!

MOTHER: That heavy thumping that irrigates and nourishes the hand.

FATHER: What hand?! What in the name of God are you talking about?

MOTHER: Is the peace difficult, Father?

FATHER: *You* are making it difficult.

MOTHER: Will the children be able to become useful citizens?

FATHER: Is there no rest?

MOTHER: Life is a stream.

FATHER: Shut up! The war is over. The male neighbor is in repose.

MOTHER: Can things ever be as they were?

FATHER: Mother, Mother, these questions . . . Realistically, things can never be the same; but, one must hope for another path equally complacent as the one destroyed by the war, equally as thoughtless and comfortable as before the war. The best men have is that they die in their own beds while dreaming of naked women.

MOTHER: But the children, they want the illusion of usefulness.

FATHER: Damn them! Each man for himself! That they give the house a certain emotional décor, it is well. But, should they rise in expectations that weigh upon me, falling from decorative amusement, I turn a valve in my heart and cast them from my sympathies.

MOTHER: Our children—

FATHER: Not more than any who disturb me. No, Mother, I have found nothing in this life that recommends any allegiance, or the remission of self-concern in lieu of another. We get through as best we can, as it were, in a pattern unconcerned with us. Each man—a boundary, a distant land. Men attempt to perpetuate themselves with pyramids and sons, and the lies that men call history; codes of honor, custom . . .

MOTHER: If the children should hear you they would have preferred that you died in the war, that they might remember their *brave papa*.

FATHER: What do I care for their preferences?! Don't you understand that the male neighbor believes he's killed me? I am now his prisoner, jailed in his belief. I can never be seen again in public.

MOTHER: Isn't there some way to get the male neighbor gradually used to you? Might you not introduce a piece of your dandruff in his path, then a hair, a fingernail; slowly, but surely easing yourself into his awareness?

FATHER: No, no, Mother; even if it should work he would always have it on me that I killed his child. No, no, it would be too embarrassing. He could always bring it up in conversation. He'd ask to borrow my golf clubs, and I wouldn't be able to say no. Can't you see the disadvantage of it? It's too compromising. I'd be too vulnerable.

MOTHER: Always thinking of yourself!

FATHER: Mother, please, I shall need every pleasant distraction.

MOTHER: And to think, I gave up all my ketchup for this.

FATHER: I shall need to think pleasant thoughts. I shall need to be told over and over that I acted to bring peace with honor. You and the children will have to think up amusements, just as though you were caring for an incurable invalid.

MOTHER: No, no, you will have to call the male neighbor and tell him it was all a mistake. No, no, you cannot expect us to accept the inward life; the children are most taken with saluting flags. No, no, they have plans to join the Rotary Club, and the Junior Chamber of Commerce. They've been tying knots all week preparing to join the Boy Scouts, with a view of entering business.

FATHER: War munitions! My advice is for them to place their money on munitions, always an excellent return! But they must remember not to antagonize their neighbors; take it from me, I think I have a pretty good idea about community relations— and they mustn't masturbate, that's strictly a kid's game!

MOTHER: Oh, Father, do you think . . . ?

FATHER: I do, indeed; all they need to do is to learn how to tie knots and smile.

MOTHER [to herself]: ". . . tie knots and smile" . . . Oh, Father, call up the male neighbor and tell him it was all a mistake!

FATHER: He might just take that opportunity to insult me.

MOTHER: Oh, Father, try.

FATHER: Well, no, he might insult me; after all, he has every justification on his side; it's too compromising.

[The telephone begins to ring.]

FATHER: Don't answer it, it's *him;* he's reading our thoughts!

[The telephone continues to ring.]

MOTHER: We've got to answer it, if only to keep the bell from wearing out.

[The telephone continues to ring.]

FATHER: We'll be compromised.

[*The telephone continues to ring.*]

MOTHER: Father, please, it's giving me a headache. Ringing phones always make me feel like going to the bathroom.

[*The telephone continues to ring.*]

FATHER [*picking up the receiver hesitantly*]: Hello . . . Scoutmaster . . . ? Why, yes, indeed, you people do a fine job with our boys. How lovely of you to invite my boys to join. They've been practicing knot-tying; and, and, and, they have very winning smiles.—What was that?! . . . Your young daughter— "*viciously run down by your neighbor?*" . . . Did you ever think that it might've been an accident? . . . "*The deed was bigger than the motive.*" . . . Well, that's one way of looking at it; however, the courts do take into account the difference between premeditation and accident . . . No, indeed, I have no wish to defend such a vicious crime. It's indefensible! I quite agree with you, he should be drawn and quartered! . . . But, but, think of his family; surely if he has any sons they would want to join the Boy Scouts. You wouldn't keep them out just because of that? . . . Even if they had winning smiles . . . ? How about knot-tying? Every Scoutmaster's a—a sucker for knot-tying . . . Not even knot-tying. Well, here's something, the boys love to salute things, they really go for dedicating themselves in public—to *anything* . . . Then the Rotary Club and Junior Chamber of Commerce are out, too . . . ? Well, listen, suppose the murderer was willing to fill in for your little girl, a kind of substitute child?—Yes, he would wear little dresses and curtsy . . . Certainly ring curls on the sides of his head, he's bald on top . . . No, I realize it's not the same thing, the sexual difference in a grown man—body hair is disgusting on little girls. Well, it certainly is a problem. But it does seem a shame that the lives of the boys should be spoiled because their father had a little accident, a misstep, as it were . . . Oh, yes, I quite understand—in your place I should feel . . . But of course—you wouldn't be human—any red-blooded . . . My very own thoughts, "*His wife should be raped, and his sons run out of town on a rail . . .*" So glad you called; good-by . . .

[*Their sons, Percival and Oscar, are now on stage, dressed as Boy Scouts, with short pants. They stand at attention, occasionally saluting with reverent faces; and they seem to be looking, as if into the future, with a kind of upright, blank patriotism.*]

FATHER [*referring to his telephone conversation with the male neighbor*]: He knew who it was; he threatened me in the third person. [*Looking at his sons*] And I do wish those two would practice their patriotic zeal in private.

MOTHER: What are you saying?

FATHER: Their faces seem so empty of late.

MOTHER: They're looking into the future. They see stocks and bonds. We represent a humble beginning, a log cabin, so to speak.

FATHER: *Log cabin?* This is one of the best houses on the block.

MOTHER: It's symbolic. Think of us as humble peasants. We have a humble faith in the land. We don't quite understand our sons. Fate has a brilliant future in store for them. We noticed, that as children, they were saluting things. One night we found little Oscar standing at attention in his crib. Percival's first words were, "Down with the communists!"

FATHER: What has all this to do with my being threatened on the telephone?

MOTHER: The boys proved early to be more than a match for ordinary tasks. Oscar was splitting rails at six months. Percival built the very cabin he was born.

FATHER: Meanwhile, the telephone was invented, and their poor humble father became the victim of cruel threats over it.

MOTHER: Why do you insist on stealing their glory by interjecting yourself?

FATHER: But, you're making it all up.

MOTHER: "*Your majesties, your holinesses, what do you attri-*

bute your unparalleled success to?" "A keen interest in anti-communism, and an undying loyalty to personal ambition." The applause, Father, it's deafening!

FATHER: What are you saying?

MOTHER: The boys, they have reached the highest approval. Great minds are met to create new offices for the boys to fill. Countries give up their boundaries that they might merge into one country to be led by our boys. Our boys climb Mt. Everest! Our boys join a circus and water the elephants. Their greatest triumph comes in flagpole sitting. Oh, the crowds, the milling, admiring crowds! A petition is gotten up, everyone on earth signs it, asking God not to ever let the boys die. Do you see it?—From humble beginnings, a stable in Bethlehem, a log cabin in Kentucky, from a New York tenement, born of immigrant parents—the boys, the boys, sitting under a bo tree, suckled by a wolf, bringing spaghetti back from China—all from humble beginnings, and in spite of, and, and from my log cabin womb, built by their own hands—no place at the inn!

FATHER: They were both born in a hospital!

MOTHER: It's *symbolic!* They were not like other children. One could tell they were destined for greatness. Take Oscar, for instance, he was able at his birth to speak with the doctor. Percival assisted at his own birth.

FATHER: Shut up! Do you think I want to hear about them while my own life lies in ruins? You only compound my difficulties with these descriptions; promoting a most unflattering comparison.

MOTHER: The boys were hampered by a jealous father, who used scorn and humiliation to inhibit their rising expectations. Their father was an alcoholic and a spendthrift. Their poor mother was forced to support the family, and has, fortunately, come to equal enshrinement with her most noteworthy sons. The father was a child molester, and a vicious communist.

FATHER: What are you saying? I'm a victim of The Industrial Revolution.

MOTHER: Their father was in a commy-backed labor union.

FATHER: That's a lie! Their father was a victim of Alexander Graham Bell.

MOTHER: In revolutionary times their father worked with the British. But the boys crossed the Delaware and won the war against the English Bolsheviks. Then their father joined the great Indian uprising, just as the boys were going West in covered wagons.

FATHER: I'm not against the boys.

MOTHER: Their father was not a communist, just a fellow traveler, soft on them, a dupe.

FATHER: The boys are very accomplished, and I certainly don't mean to take anything away from them. But it's just possible that the war might start again, any minute—[*A rock comes through the window; in the background the sounds of war.*]

MOTHER: Oh, why did you have to kill the neighbor's child, she never did anything to you?

FATHER: Mother, it was an accident. You know it was an accident. You gave up all your ketchup because you believed in me.

MOTHER: But it's unfair, why should we have to suffer on account of you? The male neighbor wants you, not us. Why should we have to suffer broken windows?

FATHER: But I didn't break the window.

MOTHER: The male neighbor breaks the window instead of you. It's you he wishes to break. It isn't fair. I didn't marry you to live in a house of broken windows. I thought I'd be a queen carried about in a sedan chair; attended to, perfumed, bathed in scented oils, adored, worshiped! No, instead of bouquets, rocks are tossed through the window. You cannot expect me to go on without being worshiped. I haven't been worshiped in all the time I've been married. [*Reaching for the rock*] Look, there's a note tied to it.

FATHER: Don't read it!

MOTHER [*taking the note off the rock, beginning to read*]: It says—

FATHER: No!

MOTHER: It says, *one pound of coffee, ten tablespoons, a dozen oranges, toothpicks, if not gold, wooden, a lady's diamond watch, a bottle of aspirin, one pound of chopped meat, a bag of onions, wrinkle cream—*

FATHER: What does it say?!

MOTHER: . . . *Seven bottles of ketchup, one dust mop, and call the man about fixing the corkscrew.*

FATHER: What does it mean?

MOTHER: Why do you ask for meaning at a time like this?

FATHER: Because it may make the difference.

MOTHER: Of what?

FATHER: Between alternatives.

MOTHER: Father, stop it, stop it, I can't stand anymore!

FATHER: Perhaps it's a list of reparations, which would make right the breach in our relations; which was caused by an unfortunate accident, a misstep, as it were, leading to a rather dangerous situation having developed between ourselves and our neighbors. Perhaps you've heard of the difficulty?

MOTHER: No, Father, what is it?

FATHER: You must know what I'm talking about, it's been discussed in the house for quite sometime now. Surely, you've put two and two together . . . ?

MOTHER: What?

FATHER: I stepped on the neighbor's child. It lay in my path. I calculated: Will I be able to avoid it? No—

MOTHER: Oh, that. Yes, I've heard some talk.

FATHER: See, I knew you must have heard something.

MOTHER: Well, I couldn't help overhearing, there's been so much talk.

FATHER: I'm not accusing you of eavesdropping; I'm glad you know. You have a right to know.

[*The sounds of war, whistling shells, bombs exploding, with, perhaps, some martial music. Percival and Oscar, who have been standing at attention and saluting once in a while, now run noisily off stage in panic.*]

PART FIVE

[*A short time has passed, but the house and their clothes show that the war has been in progress since the end of part four. In the background, where appropriate, the sounds of war, battlefield voices, explosions and flashes of light; even bugles—but nothing so loud as to interfere with what is being said on stage.*]

FATHER: Well, say something!

MOTHER: All my ketchup, the aspirations of the children—and for what?

FATHER: For me . . . When times were good nobody noticed the old man who supported them. No, only songs and all manner of gay pursuit, midnight parties and garden romance . . . [*With distraction*] . . . All where the stink of roses makes an aphrodisiac of night under the uluant moon at full—though the universe were vast, we are secure . . . But, should I stumble under the weight, should a child lie in the path of the potential footfalls of my Oxfords, whilst I, stumbling under the weight of financial burden, dazed, as it were, calculating, mind you, to avert the impediment, and not only for the sentimental implication, but for the danger implied therein of falling; not to mention the male neighbor, who must take this as a call to arms. And then, the piteous choice of falling into his hands, or quickening my gait at risk of injuring my heart.

MOTHER: But what has all that to do with us?

FATHER: Don't ask me, ask the *unmoved Mover*, He's the one unmoved, even by human tears. No accidents, only human surprise at what happens . . . Forced through countless wombs we rose—cities growing out of campsites—new lands discovered, spilling—the sword and the Cross—the fungus following its nutrition! We are premeditated, not by ourselves, but by the stars!

88

MOTHER: But, man is useful, he has a need to craftsmanship. Even the rack and the gas chamber, were they not made with an eye to craftsmanship, Father? Even those to be killed dug neat graves for themselves. Man was obedient to duty in spite of the stars.

FATHER: But they did seek a way out.

MOTHER: Yet, in the end they knew the *end* had come.

FATHER: But they had to try, they might be mistaken, there might be a way out. It is possible to give up too early.

MOTHER: . . . In that death will come no matter how we choose.

FATHER: But it can be kept off for a time.

MOTHER: Yet, no matter how we choose—

FATHER: But why should we go to meet it? If it is put off for five minutes . . .

MOTHER: But it comes, squeezing five minutes into no time; time being in continual decay there's no avoiding the end.

FATHER: What are you talking about?!

MOTHER: I've forgotten. Were we entering a truth?

FATHER: Well, I wish you'd shut up and stop wasting what may be the last part of my life listening to your babble—piffle!

MOTHER: What did I say?

FATHER: That's just it, *nothing*. Here, I hoped you were leading me to suicide on philosophical steps, that final deus ex machina. But you merely make noises disguised as philosophy. Have you no loyalty at *all*? Must I continually remind you that I am in grave danger emanating from the male neighbor, who has, through the years, sought some excuse to move against me . . . Now, in the time of crisis, at the apex of danger, in the midday of despair, in the deepest hole of wretchedness, when dreams of the garden, the rose in scent—moonlight and the mistress of the sexual quest . . . Ah, ah, all that was lovely shudders, breaking like an image on a lake, so the mind cracks and is made of disconnections.

MOTHER: But the children, not to mention the mortgage, or the milkman's money, the money for the braces on Percival's teeth, the special shoes for Oscar's flat feet, their uniforms, not to mention the insurance and the new lawnmower.

FATHER: There will be a slight deferment of conveniences, to be sure. In time of hostility certain services break down. No hope for it—men called away to service. We civilians manage until the boys come home, keeping the home fires burning, so to speak. Being most careful whilst tending the fires that we don't set the house afire. Grave danger of inexperienced hands . . . Though setting the house afire, still, it is not forgotten that the very best of intentions lay at the root of the mischief. "No, no, we forgive you this time, but take care not to befoul the nest again."—Promises, surely, magnificent oaths, worthy of documentation, the brave smile, the solemn handclasp.

MOTHER: Not to mention *ketchup* as a building block toward the new reachievement.

FATHER: Not to mention the garden, and the rose in scent, the moon at full, the werewolf at bay, and the loins at flood tide, and . . . Ah, ah, the woman described by moonlight and shadow; and, as I have said, the werewolf at bay, the dinosaurs long dead, yellow fever conquered, courtesy of the good Doctor Reed . . . Ah, ah!

MOTHER: You're not forgetting the ketchup . . . ?

FATHER: Was it springtime? A light rain falling, and the essence of rose filling the air with aphrodisiac.

MOTHER: I was striking the bottom of a ketchup bottle with the heel of my hand.

FATHER: The air fluttered with bird and blossom; and then the wind, in handsome deed, blew clean the green wood, and it rose out of the spectral fogs like a ship out of a bank of clouds . . .

MOTHER: Blop, out it came—BLOP!

FATHER: What?!

MOTHER: The *ketchup!*

CURTAIN